MORE IDEAS
for
PRAYER

---

200 SUGGESTIONS

by

Dom Hubert van Zeller

TEMPLEGATE

SPRINGFIELD, ILLINOIS

Nihil obstat
A. M. Young, O.S.B.
13 June 1966

Imprimatur
B. C. Butler, Abb. Press
15 June 1966

MORE IDEAS

for

PRAYER

To
the Sacred Heart Novitiate,
Kenwood, N.Y.

1

The duty of loving God, wrote St Augustine, is not fulfilled when it is performed as a duty. He was disposing of a widely popular myth. The doctrine which prefers a cold obedience, performed simply because it is obligatory, to the act inspired by a charitable impulse finds favour today. St Augustine would hold it to be a doctrine which can be pushed too far. Obviously to perform a good work which goes against one's inclination is more meritorious than to do it on the crest of an enthusiastic wave. But this neither canonises disinclination nor condemns enthusiasm.

If charity were to mean no more than satisfying the outward obligation, then the text about 'the letter killing and the spirit giving life' has to be reversed. Also disproved would be St Paul's exhortation to charity where he says that to speak with the tongues of angels, to have faith which moves mountains, to give away everything to the poor, and to be burned to death without the one thing which gives value to these acts would profit a man nothing.

The outward act of charity, then, cannot do duty for the inward movement of love. If love is to be a force, which it must be since God is love, it will not switch itself off when the terms of the command have been met. The tongues of fire which came upon the apostles at Pentecost would not have been necessary had no more been required than fidelity to enactments felt to be burdensome. A list of new rules would have done instead.

2

It is one thing to satisfy a law and another to live by it. Christ's command to love God and neighbour went beyond particular legislation: it pointed to a way of life. His gospel was a testament of love. It was something different from the old testament with its emphasis on the legal side of the service of God. His was a legacy exemplified by his statement that 'greater love than this no man has' than that he should give his life in the name of love. Evidently, then, the new law of love towards God and man was something more than an addition to the existing laws of religion. Our Lord was not telling us to behave in a certain way or we would be excluded from his allegiance; he was showing us the meaning of love. Once love is understood, behaviour follows suit.

The picture of Christ which we get in the gospels is not drawn from a legal system, or even from a theology, but from life. When we look at his life, we see love to be the compelling force of all that he did and said and suffered. If Christ's example is to have any relevance, it must elicit from us the same dynamic quality which animated him.

This means that Christianity is not something imposed but something awakened. The service of God is primarily an ever deepening search after charity. Though this is a quest which engages the whole man, body as well as soul, the process begins on the inside. In giving his new law to mankind, Christ was setting in motion something which was to proceed from the heart and extend to every human activity. He was not substituting one set of obligations for another.

3

Our concept of Christianity can be easily tested. Do I think of it as duties and dogmas, or as love of God and man? Do I think of Christ as the founder of a religion or as the lover of souls? Without losing our claim to orthodoxy we can know Christ only in what he did. We need also to know why he did it. It was not from a sense of duty that he founded the Church. He redeemed man not because he felt he ought to. In every activity of his, love was the inspiration. Love of the Father, love of souls.

To be moved by the sense of duty without being moved by love is like advertising a commodity without knowing what the commodity is for. The conscience which tells a man he should do this and not that is in fact, whether it knows it or not, crying out for the motive of love. If fear of going against his conscience is his sole reason for taking the line he does, a man may be upright as a human being but he is incomplete as a follower of Christ.

A man's work is important, but not as important as the reason for which he works. Suffering, praying, resisting temptation, showing compassion: these things are vastly important, but their importance derives from the spirit in which they are done. To do penance out of fear is good as far as it goes. To give alms because someone is standing at the door with a subscription list is good as far as it goes. But the principles of penance and almsgiving invite you to go all the way.

4

By focusing upon the visible we limit our visibility. If it is true that without vision a people perishes, it is true of a soul that works of charity perish for lack of this vision of love. Where the works are not the seal of love they are in danger of being nothing. Even in the natural order, in the play of the affections, love moves from the heart and the understanding to the senses. Where it begins in the senses it is likely to end in the senses, and will not be love at all.

Is this putting too high a price on love, human and devine? When the injunction is to love God with the *whole* heart, and when others are to be loved with the attention which we devote to our own wellbeing, the demand of love knows no limit. The man who says 'I do what I am supposed to do . . . don't talk to me of love' is either very foolish or very humble.

Put it this way. Love, to be the authentic inspiration of Christian action, does not have to be explicit. 'So long as you did it to one of these, the least of my brethren, you did it to me.' But, using the immediate object *as* the immediate object, love has to be there. If the immediate object were kindly treated for purposes of self-advertisement, then 'one of these' would certainly not be regarded by God as the vehicle of service to himself.

5

In St Paul's chapter on love, where he gives to the Corinthians a list of qualities which distinguish this 'more excellent way' from any other, it is significant that of charity's thirteen marks only two relate to outward conduct: boastfulness and aggressiveness. All the rest—patience, unselfishness, delight in the truth, refusal to take offense, refusal to give way to envy and the rest—are more concerned with inward dispositions than with actual conduct.

But what about St John, who says that love, to be genuine, must show itself in action? What about St James, who says that deeds are the only guarantee that there is anything behind the deeds? There is no contradiction. All three agree that, given the right attitude of mind, right conduct follows. It is our Lord's own doctrine: 'If you love me, keep my commandments.' The point is that in order to keep the commandments, a soul must first have the will to love. Where there is no will to love, there is no reason, apart from that of maintaining good order, for keeping the commandments.

'Love' says St John, 'is from God.' Two things follow from this statement. One is that it is not something worked up in himself by man. Another is that so-called charitable works need not necessarily be from God at all. Love worthy of the name begins in God and finds its way back to him. But there can be a lot of floundering about in between.

6

Here is an anomaly which deserves the closest attention. Though love is not only the operative cause of man's existence but also the final end of his endeavour—is, in other words, the whole meaning of his life—it is nevertheless love which is the main cause of man's moral failure.

While it is only through love that man achieves the wholeness for which he is designed, it is through his false interpretation of love that this wholeness is denied him. God sets a man off on a course that leads to freedom, truth, happiness; man, impatient at the slowness of the pace, and giving obscurity of vision as his excuse, deviates from this course.

Without love, man can never shake off the demands made by self; but so urgent is self to shake off the demands made by God that the terms of love are rejected. Longing for freedom, the soul mistakes the false freedom for the true. In the service of God there is liberty; in the service of self there is slavery. Man naturally wants to love without restraint and to be loved in return. The instinct is right, and, properly handled, leads to human fulfillment. Where man goes wrong is in his understanding of restraint. By letting loose the wrong powers he restrains the right ones.

7

True human love has this in common with the love of God: it does not make reservations. Because it is the giving of self, it is forgetful of self. Not until someone has been in love, either with another human being or with God, can he know what it is to leave himself out of the picture. He understands without being told that self-sacrifice is essentially bound up with what he is experiencing.

Self-sacrifice is not a necessary evil which love cannot avoid; it is love's appropriate expression, and therefore a good. Where love is found at its best, whether human or divine, the laying down of self is welcomed as an act of homage, as an opportunity, as the meeting of a summons. Where this element of voluntary self-sacrifice is lacking, even though occasions of realizing it have not yet arisen, the love is incomplete. Is in fact not love at all.

The perfection of love as found in our Lord is our model here. His self-giving showed itself in going to the full length both in obedience to the Father and in the terms of man's redemption. The practical implication of this twofold example is not hard to see. We in our degree have somehow to reflect Christ's willingness to follow the Father's will, whatever the cost, and to put life at the disposal of others. Only so shall we attain to liberty, to personal completeness, to peace.

8

If we water down Christ's commandment about love, or restrict the application of his example, we as surely rule out our chances of psychological fulfillment as we would rule out our chances of physical completeness by cutting off our own heads. In abject poverty we can be complete human beings, as we can also when in opposition to prevailing standards or when deprived of outlet to our aspiration, but we cannot be complete if we do not take God's view of love.

God *is* love, so he must be right about it. It is for him to lay down the manner of its expression, not for us. Left to ourselves we allow greed rather than grace to determine the manner of love's realization. So the answer is to let the Holy Spirit dictate, and to silence the voice of the senses.

If St John had said, 'supernatural love is from God,' he would have stated only the obvious. But in the unqualified use of the word 'love' he was telling us that, unless it is proved to be carnal, love must be accepted as spiritual. At the level of human emotion, love has the makings of something holy.

9

The strongest argument for the existence of legitimate satisfaction is the fact that God has planted in the human heart a need for it. Though man may deny himself, delude himself, subject himself to any number of physical or psychological substitutions, he knows that each of his appetites has its proper object, and that the object is attainable. The search for truth which is a necessary element in everyone's life does not exist to be frustrated. If the eye looks for beauty there must be something in the world worth looking at. If the faculty of laughter has been given to man there must be something in the world to laugh at.

The deepest of human needs is for the union which is brought about by love. Only in this union is man's never-ending quest for self-fulfillment effected. Some understand this more clearly than others, but one aspect of it which his experience teaches everyone is that the desire is infinite. Nothing short of union with God can meet the demand of the heart, and the sooner he accepts this fact the nearer a man is to the wholeness to which he can attain in this life.

10

Though I may long to be myself, the complete individual who I am meant to be, I may have very little idea as to how this is to be achieved. The reason why I am restless, unsure of myself, envious, afraid of taking on the full responsibility of living, is that I have never entirely pledged myself to one side or the other. I am not choosing wholly according to nature or wholly according to grace.

So long as I allow myself to live two lives I must be content with half a self. Christ came to give us life, abundant life, but it had to be life in him. Once we find our lives in him we find our own full identity. Nature and grace come together in the Christ-life, and there is no longer a conflict.

The idea that a wholehearted service of God has a de-humanising effect on people is bound to be wrong. Humanity was at its richest in Christ. Christ came to redeem and sanctify humanity, not to overlay it and restrict its development with the demand of religion. The redeemed man is entitled to human completeness. The saint is the finished product, the wholly balanced individual.

11

The man who is not a saint can, though he is redeemed and is trying to co-operate with the grace of sanctification, so hanker for those satisfactions which prevent him from being his real self as to split himself in two. He wants two things at once: he hopes to compensate for not being himself, and, finding that compensations are no use, he expects to be able to do without natural satisfactions altogether.

Only when created pleasures are not looked to as an escape can they be enjoyed as they are meant to be enjoyed. Taken as coming from God, and not as an indemnity to make up for the hardness of God's service, they help towards personal realization. Creation is designed to minister to man, not to get in the way of his finding himself.

God offers us our true selves, and something inside us shrinks from taking possession. We are afraid of being committed. We see what we might become, what one part of us longs to become, yet we feel it will be easier if we go on as we are. What we really fear is not the wholeness which can be ours for the asking, but the trials and sufferings which we know must accompany this wholeness. This much we have learned of Christ, and of those who follow him, that the fuller the personality the more searching the passion.

12

Love brings out love. Truth brings out truth. Personality brings out personality. Anyone who lays himself open to receive the wholeness of Christ becomes whole. Christ came to save, to redeem, to make whole. This is not a pun; it is a fact. Giving himself to Christ, a man becomes himself. When he redeems us, Christ gives us back ourselves larger than life—larger than the half life which we knew before.

You would think that everyone in the world would relish the idea of life in Christ with the promise of achieving self-realization. You would think this hope would be able to take the fear in its stride. You would think man could see through the argument against taking on the really worthwhile thing in life.

In order to understand the dilemma we have to go back a step and ask how the fear originates. Any psychiatrist will tell you that what most of his patients suffer from is immaturity. For one reason or another—usually because their parents have been too possessive or else by bad example and neglect have driven their children to take refuge in childhood—people resist the process of growing up.

13

Who has not met the adult who reveals his immaturity either by refusing to face the challenges of life or by covering up his lack of identity with a show of arrogance? How often do we not come across self-assertion where there is no self to assert? The alternative to living the mature life is to live in a world of fantasy and evasion.

At the mention of grown-up people living in a world of fantasy, we think at once of those who like to picture themselves as cowboys or medieval knights. It is not these to whom reference is made. The unromantic, down-to-earth, practical subject is just as liable to live in unreality. Possibly more so, because the man who is earthbound beyond a certain point, and over-reliant on practical worldly wisdom, will find it all the harder to enter by faith into the life of grace and so bring about his fullness in Christ.

'Created nature has been condemned to frustration,' writes St Paul to the Romans, 'that nature might be set free from the tyranny of corruption to share the glorious freedom of God's sons . . . we groan in our hearts, waiting for that adoption which is the ransoming of our bodies from their slavery, in Christ Jesus our Lord.'

14

In saying 'Leave me to myself, Lord, for I am a sinner,' St Peter spoke for more than he knew. It was a case of the soul drawing back from the summons to go forward and be a responsible person. Christ's answer was to tell Peter not to be afraid. The fear was as familiar a phenomenon to Christ as to any modern psychiatrist. We are told in the verse which concludes the account of the haul of fish and Peter's protest that 'when they had brought their boats to land, they left all and followed him.' So it was a crucial occasion for the others as well, not only for Peter.

William James refers to two kinds of men: the once born and the twice born. More vital than his initiation into human life is man's initiation into the altogether fuller life of the spirit. The really vital experience of his life is when a man discovers Christ. With this discovery goes the discovery of so much else. The moment of realization may come as the result of an emotional shock, but more usually the soul arrives at a new understanding of what life is all about, and how one's own part in it must be squarely faced, without any conscious climax having taken place.

Though grace can be thanked for this awakening, there is nothing mystical about it. In one way or another it happens to everyone. Not everyone accepts what the light reveals, but all get their chance. 'There is one who enlightens every soul born into the world: he was the true light.' The once born man in William James can become the twice born man if he wants to. The experience of Nicodemus tells us this.

15

The awful responsibility which is man's, and the havoc which can be made of it, is clearly stated by St John. 'He through whom the world was made, was in the world, and the world treated him as a stranger. He came to his own, but they who were his own gave him no welcome.' A man may acknowledge Christ, yet keep him at a distance. In all of us exists the fatal ability to accept and let it go at that. We believe and quickly look away.

'But all those who did welcome him he empowered to become the children of God.' The crucial act is that of giving welcome. The welcome, itself a work of grace, sets its seal on what has gone before. 'Their birth came not of human stock, not from nature's will nor man's, but from God.' So it is not enough merely to believe. 'The devils believe and tremble,' says St James. What qualifies is where the soul goes on from there.

Our Lord told the accredited religious authorities of his day that it was better to have no knowledge at all than to have the kind of knowledge which did nothing. 'So with faith,' says St James, 'if it does not lead to action it is in itself a lifeless thing.' So also with charity: the charity which is sterile is no charity. The light dawns interiorly, but this is only the start of it. It dawns in order to shine.

16

'To shine on those who live in darkness, and in the shadow of death, and to guide our feet into the way of peace.' This was spoken in prophecy by Simeon of him who was to be the light of the world. 'In your light,' the psalmist had said to the Lord, 'we shall see light.' Just as divine light, personified in Christ, came down upon earth not merely to burn in secret but to enlighten, so again its function has to be repeated when it reflects itself in the person of man.

No gift that is given us, says St Thomas, is for our own exclusive use. If whatever good we possess is to be communicated to others, the problem confronting the individual is the manner of communication. Back, now, to the postulate considered earlier: it is only by knowing my true self that I can know how to make my specific contribution to others, to mankind, to the life of the world.

If as a Christian I cannot be a parasite—our Lord's parable of the true vine tells us that—I cannot as a member of the human race so insulate myself as not to influence my fellow members. 'The whole of nature,' says St Paul to the Romans, 'groans all the while in a common travail.' We are all in it together, mutually assisting one another in the process of development, and just as we have noted the individual's progress towards maturity so here we must recognize a corporate demand. Mankind never ceases to strain, against every kind of obstacle which materialism puts in its way, to reach full stature in Christ.

17

Just like the man who knows where his fulfilment lies but fights against it, the world races faster and faster in the hopes of outdistancing its prophets and silencing their voice. Whenever it hears the word of reproach, it points to the way it has used the gifts of God for the benefit of man. It cites health services, old age relief, educational opportunities extended to emergent nations, systems of food distribution.

The social justice which is sought in the name of Christ must receive the blessing of Christ. Charity, even if they are afraid to mention the name of Christ as they extend it, cannot go unrewarded. But what if good works are purely secular works? What if economics and politics have prior claim to consideration than the gospel? What if public morality is seen in terms of statistics, hygiene, national prestige, instead of how individual souls are working out their salvation?

Secondary ends, pursued as substitutes for the end itself, delay the process of growing up. No progress which is not spiritual progress can, as it were by force, achieve maturity. Our Lord said that a man must become as a little child if he would enter the kingdom, and perhaps the world may have to learn what this means before it reaches full stature. The world will not like having to go back on what it is teaching today.

18

The Christian solution is the only one, and in essence the Christian solution is love. Every Christian would admit in principle the policy of love, but most Christians would make qualifications when it comes to drawing up a program of love's expression. 'The charity of Christ urges us': so far so good. But we do not want to be pinned down. We do not even want, some of us, to bring Christ into it by name.

Christians cannot be humanitarians and leave out the humanity of Christ. To meet the problem of human rights without charity is like treating a sick foal with a car wash: it does not improve the animal's health or help it to become a horse but only brings up a shine and makes the benefactor feel good.

So charity is not the reward which is given to the deserving: it is the motive behind the giving. The motive is placed in our souls by God, and it is this which makes us what we are. It is this, since it is God himself, which makes us lovable to God. By charity we develop our likeness to him; we bring out in ourselves his image.

19

What is known as the doctrine of spiritual childhood might equally well be called the doctrine of psychological maturity. By reflecting the child's trust and love, a man grows into fulness of life in Christ. It means forswearing the false securities of the world and the suspicions born of uncharity. Because the child gives love and expects it, not because children are attractive or ignorant of the world's ways, the child is put before us as an example.

'He that humbles himself shall be exalted.' In the measure that we learn the lesson of childhood we advance both spiritually and psychologically. But where the child is humble because he knows nothing of pride, the man is humble because his love has rejected pride. Sooner or later the man who loves God discovers that pride is an illusion. He discovers that it only makes for humiliation.

The man who perseveres in prayer becomes humble not because he plans to be but because his experience makes him so. Seeing more clearly than others the implication of love, he sees with dreadful clearness how far short he falls in response. Indeed unless his love is as trusting as it is humble he may find himself crushed by the sense of failure. The line which divides the searing pain of humility from the abandon of despair is not always easy to see. It is drawn by the will. If the feelings try to draw it, the line will wave to right and left and disappear into the darkness.

If in the last analysis the whole of virtue lies in love and its direction—*ordinavit in me caritatem* as we get it in the Canticle —then the whole of sin lies in the misappropriation of love. It is more than a negation; it is a reversal. Not only is a good turned into an evil, but the giver of all good is robbed of what he alone can give.

20

When a man sins, he takes something which represents God's love and turns it over to the love of self. God is offering him a gift, but because man is ashamed of the reason why he wants it, and of the use he is going to make of it, the gift changes character. As it is grasped, it becomes the opposite of what it is meant to be. Man having claimed it for his own, having removed it from where it belongs, is saddled with it until he says he is sorry and gives it back. Guilt is then turned into love, and the sin against love is lost in the infinite mercy of God.

So if it is God who 'orders charity in me', it is I who must take the blame for disordering it. Nobody else has power to disorder my love. Nobody else can steal from God the thing I want, and give it to me. It is I who steal, and it is always because I have wanted an aspect of love for myself. Since this is so of every sin that can be committed, it will be understood why such stress is given here to the need of reading love right.

21

Charity towards people manifests itself in any number of ways: compassion, forgiveness, trust, loyalty, the corporal and spiritual works of mercy. 'Bear ye one another's burdens, and so you shall fulfil the law of Christ.' If this rule is to be followed according to its intention, the true Christian thinks less of the other man's burden than of his claim to love. Charity to one's fellow men expresses itself first in understanding, and then in lightening their load.

Charity towards God also manifests itself in a number of ways: obedience, fidelity to the commandments, suffering, faith, hope, prayer. Since man is liable to make mistakes in each of these responses we need to safeguard ourselves as far as possible. The powers of evil are as much interested in seeing us deviate in our performance of virtue as they are in seeing us consent to the seductions of vice.

Where some would hold that the elimination of the vices is a necessary preparation for the cultivation of the virtues, we believe that to adopt the opposite order produces the better result. To wait till the vices are under control is to wait for ever. More satisfactory is to aim straight at the virtues, which, given half a chance, will sublimate the vices. This approach seems more in line with the gospel teaching as illustrated by the parables of the talents, the seed, and the leaven. The gospel is essentially positive in its learning.

22

Charity's primary articulation, and the most direct, is that of worship. Its secondary expression has fellow human beings as its object. This much at least, assuming that people read the New Testament, is common knowledge. 'The first commandment,' said our Lord, 'is to love the Lord your God with all your heart, with all your soul, with all your mind and with all your strength; and the second is like unto this: love your neighbour as yourself. There is no commandment greater than these.'

When God commands something, he gives the grace of obeying as perfectly as it lies in us to obey. Fidelity to this two-fold commandment induces the mentality which is not content with going through the motions of worship but which actually loves in its worship, which is not content to treat others charitably but which actually loves them.

Though we know nothing of our Lady's prayer beyond what we can get out of her attitude when addressed by the angel Gabriel, we judge instinctively that to her the idea of worship was not something which had to be forced. Though we know little more of her relations with other people, we judge instinctively that she had the interests of others at heart without having to put them there. Did she visit her cousin Elizabeth because it would have looked heartless if she had not? Did she come to the rescue of the bridal pair at Cana because she wanted to exact from herself a high standard of thoughtfulness?

23

While we cannot always feel, either towards God or towards others, what we want to feel, we must be careful not to despise the desire. By bringing the ideal of charity down to the level of our own experience of it, we can forget that the ideal exists in spite of us. Though it would be a mistake, and would show a lack of truth, to claim a fervour which is not ours, it would be still more mistaken and untruthful to decry affective charity.

It is because the ideal of affective charity is for most of us less immediately relevant than the practice of effective charity that so much space in spiritual books is devoted to the work of the will rather than to the work of the heart. And rightly so: look after faith, and you can leave feelings to look after themselves. So much more of life is spent in darkness than in light, in coldness than in warmth, that a doctrine which concerns the difficulties of prayer and the obstacles to Christian charity is more needed than a doctrine which treats only of the comforts along the way.

'Blessed are they that have not seen but have believed,' is accordingly the text which souls will need to keep within reach when they embark upon the spiritual life. Much of their journey towards God will be done alone, without comfort, and much of their relationship with others will be frought with disappointment. The encouragement which keeps them on their way will have to come through trust and hope. They must learn to live with non-comprehension and misunderstanding or they will never get anywhere.

24

Loneliness is the trial which tests the soul's correspondence both with God and with man. Since the Christian's treatment of others corresponds pretty accurately to his treatment of God, we can examine various facets of the divine relationship before going on to consider some of the spiritual implications in the relationship between man and man.

First there is the question of God's presence. We know that God is everywhere about us, that it is a loving and not an accusing presence, that we can turn to him at any time and in any place, and that he is our 'protector and our strength'. This said, we know too that his presence does not normally make itself felt, and that sometimes we have to do violence to ourselves to believe that it is there at all.

This labour of trust, continuing our search for a reality of which the senses give no evidence, constitutes the essential burden of our prayer. But if God were not a hidden God, and if we could enjoy his presence as intimately and perceptibly as we enjoy the companionship of our friends, what would be the point of it? Certainly we would have no right to talk about faith.

25

Since, as already suggested, the way of prayer is more often the way of dry faith than of felt love, we must be sure that we know what faith means in this context. It means allowing grace to work its unquestioned and unqualified way in the soul. To think of it as a simple act of trust which leaves everything in God's hands, and makes no further demands, is to have a false idea of its purpose. That faith should go on demanding is very much part of it.

Faith is not given us so that we can enjoy the comfortable assurance that we have done all we can. In most souls it has almost the opposite effect: it makes them feel they have nothing to offer except their sinfulness, and at the same time they cannot see any way of putting themselves right. Faith is not made for comfort, and those who expect it to be a cushion will find it is swept from under them when they most want to sit on it.

St Paul, echoing Osee, proclaims faith to be that by which the just man lives. It is not that on which the weak man leans. Faith is neither a substitute for thinking, a vehicle of mystical experience, or a religious formula which covers everything and might be equated with fatalism. The virtue which is chosen by God to be the means of a man's salvation—'this is eternal life: to know you who alone are truly God, and Jesus Christ whom you have sent'—must elicit more from the soul than merely the consent to be anaesthetized.

26

The prayer of faith is not a cosy-chat prayer. There is an astringency about it, conveyed particularly by this loneliness which we have mentioned, which souls must get used to if they are to persevere in it. That they should have to make the pilgrimage unaccompanied by their fellows is bad enough, but that they should lack the companionship of him for whom the pilgrimage is undertaken is infinitely worse.

Nor is such loneliness confined to the times of prayer. The ache of it is felt from the moment of getting up in the morning until the time of going to bed. The most unlikely occasions are those when it is felt most. For instance when in the company of young people who are enjoying themselves, and who include one in their enjoyment, there is felt to be a vacuum in the heart which no amount of young people can ever fill.

There is no fighting off these periods of spiritual and social isolation. But what can be fought off is the mood of self-pity which they can easily engender. Once a man is deluded into feeling sorry for himself it is twice as hard to get the spiritual life going again in him. The reason is not hard to see. The life of faith has God as its centre of focus. Self-commiseration leaves no room for God; its whole interest is directed inwards. Self-commiseration is such an absorbing luxury that it cannot interest itself in the affairs of others. It is envious if others are seen to be worse off.

27

Still on the subject of faith and the trial of loneliness, it is by resorting to more prayer, and not less, that the test is met. The activity in which the pain of God's absence is most felt is the activity which brings the strength to endure the loss. It is like the spear of Achilles which heals as it wounds. Prayer does not lessen the pressure, because in the providence of God the pressure is not meant to be lessened, but with it comes the light to see how loneliness must play a necessary part in the spiritual life.

In order to benefit by this light, the soul does not have to meditate upon the particular pressure of the moment—the less we meditate upon our trials the better, or we shall find ourselves giving in under them—but rather to concentrate on faith and on the mercy of God. Love seems out of reach for the time being, and hope seems empty. Acts of love and hope are made, but made with difficulty. It is only because of faith that they can be made at all.

28

By faith we can make concessions to the sense of being cut off and not belonging. We can come to respect it as a vocation to solitude. People do not realize nearly enough the possible advantages of loneliness: how it can be turned to the service of contemplation. Prayer shows them the openings, and how to make use of opportunity. Without a certain measure of solitude, and therefore of loneliness, it is difficult to see how interior prayer can really flourish.

But in all this we must avoid the temptation to generalize and be pontifical. No definite rules can be laid down for the prayer of faith—or, if it comes to that, for any other kind of prayer. Each soul has to meet the trials of this particular state as best he can. He is never sure that his prayer will stay the same for two days running. There seems no pattern, no continuity, no reality. There is only the purpose, remembered from long ago, which must be clung to whatever happens.

Accordingly the soul cannot submit material for prayer beforehand nor give an account afterwards for what has been going on. Most will prefer to pray while Mass is in progress, because then at least there is something concrete and actual with which they can unite. Apart from this attraction, which can become a hunger bordering upon exaggeration, there is no knowing what is happening, why it is happening, and when it will cease happening.

29

About the prayer of faith, all that directors and writers can do is to say what has helped *them,* and to hope that this will help other people. They can outline a course which they believe to be safe, but even here it is possible to mistake their meaning and go off at a tangent. Directors and writers can point out the pitfalls, can turn the soul's gaze towards divine things, can back up the argument with quotations from authentic sources. But they cannot advance the soul one step unless the soul decides to take it.

Neither the written nor the spoken word can of itself give

peace: it can only tell where it can be found. There are souls who look to spiritual reading and conferences for more than they are designed to provide. The important thing is what happens in the will when the doctrine has been understood.

It is sometimes even necessary to detach oneself from a slavish adherence to a director or favourite author. External helps can become hindrances when they have the effect of forcing the soul into a mould. Spiritual advice is meant to dispose the soul for prayer and not to dictate terms. The prayer of many souls is distracted by worries as to whether the directions are being followed. The summons of grace, which is normally responded to by pursuing one's own attraction in prayer, cannot survive if the summons to follow a cramping directive is given priority.

30

Souls very soon discover that their prayer cannot be counted upon to follow a pattern for any length of time. Because of this—and one's prayer can even vary from day to day —it would seem a waste of time to prepare a meditation overnight. Yesterday's *schema* will this morning either engross the reasoning and imaginative faculties to the exclusion of simple faith, or it will be felt to have no bearing upon the impulse of grace and the attraction which is felt at the moment. So why bother? Far better to use the time which is put aside for collecting material, in praying according to the material provided here and now by grace.

Once we admit that there is no knowing how grace will act next, we can adapt ourselves to whatever prayer God sends. If we expect a certain form of prayer, making up our minds to be exact in the handling of it, we are liable to miss the kind of prayer which God wants of us. Characteristic of the prayer of faith is not to know what is happening, why it is happening, when it will cease happening. Except indirectly, such a prayer cannot be effectively prepared for.

In proportion as proximate preparation is felt to be unsatisfactory, remote preparation is all the more necessary. By this is meant the effort to acquire the habit of recollection, the good use of leisure and solitude, the avoidance of deliberate imperfection. Obviously the man who lets entertainment, conversation, physical fitness dominate his day will find himself at a loss when he comes to the set times of prayer.

31

The grace of prayer is not something miraculous. It is not a state which, like a hypnotic trance, comes on and off. It is there if we want it, and it will develop if we take steps to safeguard it. Always it remains God's free gift, but on the authority of St John of the Cross it is unthinkable that God should deny the grace to those who want it.

Because it is God's free gift, and not of our own shaping, it is a mistake to judge it by psychological or scientific standards. Just as God's grace does not have to wait upon a list of points to be meditated next day, so it does not confine itself to the findings of analysis. When it seemed that the people of Nazareth were thrusting his passion upon him before the time, Jesus 'passed through the midst of them and went his way'. Grace in the same way does not allow itself to be forced.

The only grace which concerns us is the grace which is coming to us now, and if this defies analysis so also do the graces which we have had or might be having. The clause in the *Our Father,* 'Give us this day our daily bread,' contains a statement as well as a petition. It tells us that our need can be met from day to day so long as we trust and accept the bread God gives us.

32

The idea of getting one's daily bread from God is the guiding principle of a saint's life. Most of us either restrict its meaning or pay little attention to it. It covers the response to suffering, the resistance of temptation, the recognition of God's will, the readiness to trust in divine providence. It is inherent in the concept of prayer.

The saint does not tell God what sort of bread is best, does not worry about how tomorrow's will be delivered, does not upset himself because he has wasted some of yesterday's. The saint does not plan his prayer-life any more than he plans other aspects of life. He knows that God is planning it. The saint does not investigate the rubble of his prayer when it is over. He leaves all that to God.

That he will meet with frustration in his prayer effort, as he will in almost every other enterprise he undertakes, does not deter the saint. Frustration, like loneliness, is allowed for. The spiritual life would be incomplete without it. But there is no reason to be morose about this, still less to be bitter. Bitterness and cynicism have no place in the spiritual life. There is all the difference between being moved to rebellion and being guilty of resentment.

33

Very different from earlier expressions of devotion, the prayer of faith taxes only two faculties: intellect and will. If it were kept going by the activity of the emotions there would be less difficulty in estimating its quality. But precisely because it *is* faith, its value has to be kept out of sight. The impulse which moves it is grace, and natural activity plays little part in it. Natural activity, never altogether suspended except in strictly supernatural prayer, has quite enough to do in merely hanging on and bidding for perserverance.

No wonder God keeps the soul in this kind of prayer for longer than in any hitherto: there is more of grace in it, more of himself. He can arrange it and re-arrange it as it suits him without interference on the soul's part. So rather than try to bring their prayer under the microscope, souls who are in the way of faith would be advised to let go and commit questions of success or failure in the spiritual life to the care of God.

The prayer of faith and the life of faith develop correspondingly. This is a more important consideration than may appear. All would probably admit, whatever their intention of orientating themselves towards God, that their lives run along two different paths: one religious, the other secular. The religious or spiritual path is traced in terms of prayer, the sacraments, Mass, devotions and so on; the secular or material path is simply the rest of life. In an ordinary well-ordered Christian life these paths, though parallel, are to a greater or lesser degree distinct and separate. The prayer of faith, by inducing the habit of faith in everyday life, narrows the gap. In the case of the saints the two paths merge into one.

34

We are divided beings. We have lost the integrity enjoyed by our first parents. Our religion is in one part of us, and our management of affairs, our recreation, our contacts with people are in another. For most of the time the two parts seem to be in opposition. But this is all wrong, and the spiritual life should put it right. The prayer of faith, if we are generous enough to persevere in it, does in fact put it right.

Or see it this way: the multiplicity engendered by pre-occupation with self gives place to the simplicity which looks for God alone. Material concerns are attended to, but not as being the end-all of human existence. They are even taken seriously, but not as seriously as the things which relate to God. When the prayer of faith is really doing its work, the things of every day are seen in relation to eternity.

More than this, God is seen to reveal himself in material things. Life is no longer schizophrenic, living at two levels and searching for two different satisfactions, but unified. God is seen to be working through his creation, and his creatioin is accepted for what it is. In the last analysis there is really only one point of view which the Christian can adopt, but the surest way by which he can adopt it is the way of faith. That is why prayer is to him a necessity.

35

People who, despite the call to unity in faith, imagine they can get along with one foot in each camp are taking great risks. Sooner or later, though without having deliberately chosen to turn down grace or perhaps even noticed its stages, they will find themselves consulting their own interests and waiving those of God.

The issue cannot be evaded indefinitely: 'You cannot serve two masters.' God gives souls the grace to be his servants, not his nodding acquaintances. God is not one who can be left to come a bad second—with 'mammon' coming first.

To prevent mammon from assuming the mastery, we must pray for the light to see where we are choosing apart from God.

So blinding are material values that we can allow ourselves to deviate from our proper course before we see the seriousness of the situation. In case it should be thought that the prayer of faith debars the soul from making requests in prayer it must be said at once that this is not so. Since the will is here engaged more than any other faculty, there is nothing to prevent the will desiring what is needful, and expressing its desires as often and as forcefully as it feels moved to do.

36

In the literature of the spirit there is a tendency to look down upon the prayer of petition as being in some way inferior. The idea that petition is unworthy of spiritual people, who should be content to praise God without asking for favours, could lead to some bleak errors fortunately condemned by the Church. If it is a prayer more used by beginners than by the advanced, this should not dismay us: advancement in the spiritual life is only the right use of what we begin with. We begin by praying according to the attraction that is given us by the spirit, and this is what we go on doing until the end.

It may be more noble and meritorious to hang on by your eyelids in faith than to recite a litany of requests, but if God gives you the light to make requests it is no good pretending to a more austere kind of prayer. You have to pray as you are moved to pray, even if this is not the prayer which you would design for yourself if you were the Holy Spirit. So you can forget about what is nobler and more meritorious, and take your own prayer for what it is. You will probably find that it is for the most part, directly or indirectly, asking.

And why not? Our Lord blesses such prayer, urges us to persevere in it if we want to be heard, pledges himself and his Father to reward it. The *Our Father* petitions that God's name be praised, that his kingdom may come, that his will be done, that he give us our daily bread, that he forgive us our sins, that he lead us out of temptation, and that he deliver us from evil. Seven requests in the most perfect of all prayers.

37

Those who charge the prayer of petition with selfishness

should bear in mind first that to pray *without* an element of self-interest would require an altogether extraordinary grace, and second that the very act of asking God for something pays him the compliment of our dependence upon his power to grant it. So in his petitions man gives praise to God, and in his praises he implies petitions.

'Let your petitions be made known to God,' is the advice which St Paul gives the Ephesians, and in almost all his letters the apostle shows his respect for the prayer of petition by begging his readers to remember various intentions of his. To Timothy he recommends the kind of widow who 'continues in supplications night and day.' St James points to the petition which Elias addressed to the Lord for dry weather 'and it did not rain for three years and six months.'

The psalms are full of petitions—sixteen in the *Miserere* alone—and to round off the argument we have our Lord making frequent requests of the Father. If our Lord can pray for his friends, for his Church, for the forgivenness of his persecutors, and even, if it should be the Father's will, for a cessation of his own sufferings, we have all the precedent we want.

38

To exclude petition from our prayers as a venture of lofty detachment would mean leaving out at least two thirds of the Mass and re-wording the form of the sacraments. One wonders where those souls get their prayer-material and incentive who primly proclaim that they 'never like asking for favours . . . the good Lord knows what is needed, and can safely be left to use his own judgment.' Of course he can, but what if he is holding the gift until it is prayed for?

Where it is a question of grace, it is easy to see how prayer can be the condition of its granting. But material and temporal benefits can also be conditional. If this principle holds good, it is humbling to speculate as to the amount of help we could have had if only we had responded to the impulse of grace which urged us to ask for it. There must be many miracles which go unworked because people are either too hesitant or too lazy to plead for them.

God has the whole supernatural world to draw from, and for one reason or another we are shy of getting him to use it.

God is master of the possible and the impossible alike, and we dare not expect more of him than the probable. The saints are not so squeamish, consequently their prayers are answered. They believe what they are told about praying with faith, so their faith is—in ways surprising to us—rewarded.

39

One reason why our petitions are not more often granted may be that they are loaded with qualifications designed to soften our possible disappointment. Confidence in the power of prayer is bound to suffer if we cover in advance the reasons which God may have for rejecting our request. We do not have so to frame our petitions as to ensure that God does not, if he has to refuse us, lose face. It is in any case assumed that the person praying means to accept God's will whatever the outcome, so why not make prayer as forthright as we can?

The warning not to be presumptuous in our prayer, not to be greedy for favours, can have an inhibiting effect. People can begin to wonder whether they are justified in asking for health when they are ill, for help when they are in trouble, for vindication when they are falsely accused. In his lifetime our Lord was pestered for help and miracles, and there is no evidence that he disapproved of it. The evidence is all the other way: he recommended perserverance in pestering, and rewarded it.

The only conditions which our Lord required for the working of his miracles were that people should 'have faith' and that they 'sin no more'. He expected gratitude, as we know from the incident of the ten lepers, but even this was not laid down as a quality on which the miracle would depend. He wanted people to ask, continue asking, have faith and turn away from sin.

40

If requests are granted on such easy terms, forgiveness is almost easier to obtain. All you have to do, as the parable of the steward and the debtor shows, is to forgive other people. There were even occasions when our Lord forgave sins without being asked to do so. He saw that the disposition of love was there, and rewarded it with plenary pardon. 'Because she has loved much' he said of the penitent woman, 'much has been forgiven her.' 'Go your way' he said to those whose faith was guarantee of love and penitence, 'your sins are forgiven.'

The mercy of God is something which can be counted upon when everything else about him seems uncertain. When a preacher once proclaimed that if the fatherhood of God were understood there would be no need to worry about hell, he was thought to be employing oratorical licence. But was he? In this changing world a father's readiness to forgive his children is about the only constant left.

In the whole psalter there is only one psalm which repeats the same statement in its every verse. Twenty-seven times in the 135th psalm the refrain occurs: 'For his mercy is everlasting'. Whatever else we are doubtful about in our requests to God, we cannot go wrong in asking for mercy. On the showing of Old and New Testament alike, there is nothing that God is more willing to grant.

41

It is unfortunate that prayer has to have labels tied to it: the prayer of praise and the prayer of petition; discoursive prayer and the prayer of simple regard; illuminative and unitive prayer; liturgical, meditative, devotional, contemplative and passive prayer. It is unfortunate partly because it makes for the study of prayer rather than for its practice, and partly because the labels are misleading. The implication is that there is no overlapping, and that the soul mounts from one to another form of prayer in ordered progression.

It would be most cramping to the spirit if the soul who was in the way of contemplation felt obliged to stifle the impulse to use words. Or if someone whose prayer was liturgical could not bring himself to make a novena. Categories are best forgotten if they limit the soul's flexibility. Souls should always be ready to change their prayer at the movement of grace, praying in the way God gives them to pray and not in the way which looks all right in the book but which does not work when they try it.

It makes it simpler if we think of the prayer which we offer to God as partaking of the prayer which he offers to himself. The prayer which passes between the divine persons of the Trinity is echoed in the prayer which issues from the Trinity to man, and through man, passes back again to the Trinity. When we fully grasp the fact that our prayer finds its origin and term in God, we are likely to pay less attention to the classifications of prayer. What does it matter whether we are praying actively or passively, mentally or vocally, so long as we are the reverberating channels which we are meant to be of God's prayer which is going back to him. 'The word which goes forth from my lips,' says the Lord, 'must not return to me void.'

42

While the relationship between the persons of the Blessed Trinity remains always the same, the relationship as expressed by prayer between ourselves and God is always changing. At times we are united in our prayer with God, and then at times we drift away and do not even try to be recollected. God makes allowance for our variations of mood, and for the circumstances which occasion them, but he can hardly be expected to approve of the restlessness which looks for new experience or the laziness which denies him our perseverance.

What fluctuations there are in our prayer must come as the work of grace and not as the result of our own choosing. Granted that we have chosen the life of prayer, and do not consciously go back on the decision, there is in point of fact very little choosing to be done. We discover quite early on that experimenting in different ways of prayer brings us up against a blank wall. There is no surer rule in the spiritual life than that we have to pray in the only way we can or not at all.

These alternations which we all experience between darkness and light, between dryness and fervour, are extremely good for us. The uncertainty of the course embarked upon elicits the authentic act of faith which is necessary to all true prayer. The characteristic of experimentalism is not faith but speculation, and there is a great difference between the two.

43

In instructing her nuns on prayer, St Teresa says that however contemplative they are, or think they are, they must always be ready to fall back for a time to more active forms of prayer. Much better to humble oneself and meditate upon the mysteries of the rosary than to play the mystic and find oneself mooning about in space.

The question now arises as to how one kind of blank can be distinguished from another. How can we know that the sense of being blocked is the work of grace and not the result of our own stupidity? Listlessness and distaste are nothing to go by, because these seem to be inherent in either alternative. Nor is the desire to escape into worldly distraction a valid test, because again this accompanies both conditions.

The issue turns upon whether the will decides to keep in operation or to let matters slide and not bother any more. One may feel bored by the whole subject of prayer, one may yearn for dissipation, one may even wish that one had not pledged oneself to the spiritual life, but if the determination to go ahead with the effort to pray remains intact then the prevailing impasse is of grace and one is not to blame. In support of this there is the consideration 'Would the fact that my prayer is a blank disturb me at all if it were occasioned by my indifference? Would I not be indifferent to how far it was my own fault?'

44

The danger of doing nothing in our prayer, and pretending we are leaving God free to work his will in us, is matched only by that of thinking that we must do all and that God need do nothing but give his approval. There is an axiom which runs: 'Without God, we cannot; without us, God will not.' It is of primary importance that this be understood. If the balance between the two presumptions is to be kept—the one presuming upon God's industry with no co-operation from us, the other upon our own industry with only a token co-operation from him—the inter-relation must be grasped between grace and human effort.

It is not quite a case of God helping those who help themselves, nor yet of those helping God who do not help themselves. Rather it is doing everything possible at a human level, while leaving the direction of the work, the manner of it and the outcome, to God. Looked at in this way, the prayer of faith has no part with either the inertia of fatalism or the busy multiplicity of those who see spirituality as the display of energy.

While there may not be the same intentness about it as

there is, for example, in the prayer of forced acts, the prayer of faith is not without its tensions. The sheer effort to hang on is taxing enough, and if the expenditure of energy is more subtle than in other spiritual exercises it is none the less real for that.

45

Though fidelity to prayer may seem to lead only into deeper darkness, it is in reality the surest means of enlightenment. For confirmation it is useless to examine the prayer itself—since there is nothing to be seen—but not so useless to look at what is going on in the soul outside prayer time. As the result of such prayer as we have been considering the soul acquires an understanding of human conduct which can hardly be acquired otherwise.

Matters which before appeared morally indifferent, or beyond the range of the soul's grasp, now become clearly pertinent questions of right and wrong. The horizon, seen in virtue of the prayer of faith which itself seems to see nothing, is no longer blurred. In forming practical judgments the soul comes to enjoy an assurance which is strangely at variance with the uncertainty which is felt interiorly.

While no amount of interior confusion is likely to obscure this clarity of judgment, sin would prejudice it in no time. St Paul describes how sin, when continued in, delivers up the sinner to the curse of possessing a 'reprobate sense' and how his perceptions, desires and values are vitiated. Sin not only disturbs but falsifies: it turns moral assessments so far away from the truth that a sincere conversion is needed if the right perspectives are to be regained.

46

So great is the power of grace that even those who have deliberately failed, who have seen the light and then resisted, can yet be restored to the full life of love. They can even rise higher than they were before, and enjoy a clearer vision than ever. But for this to happen there has to be a difinite catharsis of the spirit. King David is of course the classic example. When those who stand in high favour with God fall into serious sin, they must know utter humiliation before they can start mounting to their former state and once again enjoy their vision of truth.

Dante's experience points the same moral: infidelity followed eventually by mystical insight scarcely equalled in St John of the Cross. What written lines penetrate further than those from the concluding cantos of *Il Paradiso?* 'Fixing my gaze upon eternal light/ I saw enclosed within its depth,/ bound up with love together in one volume/ the scattered leaves of all the universe:/ substance and accidents, and their relations/ together fused in such a way/ that what I speak of is one simple flame.'

The points to notice in the above quotation are that it is love which brings about the work, and that the work is seen in unity and simplicity. This is St Benedict's experience repeated, and Dame Julian's anticipated. Whether the whole of God's creation is seen (as St Benedict saw it) in a ball of light, or (as Dame Julian of Norwich saw it) no bigger than a hazelnut, all the scattered leaves of the universe come together in one single flame of love.

47

In prayer we have always to be on our guard against profusion and the proliferation of ideas. Love tends to unity and not to multiplicity. It is nature and not grace which goes questing for new ways of expressing itself. Prayer, if it moving along the way of faith, should become increasingly simple and unadorned. Since its object is God alone, its procedure should be direct.

Feeling that they must be doing something, and that a bustling activity is the sure sign of true devotion, people can crowd their prayer with such a wealth of material that the work of grace does not get a chance. Their prayer becomes like an oriental bazaar: so much noise, colour, traffic, jostling, that it is more a matter for the nerves than for the mind.

Even those who feel drawn to tranquillity in prayer, can, from a false sense of obligation, weigh down their spirit with pious practices and holy thoughts. Material which is in itself good, can become a great obstacle when placed where it does not at the moment belong. There must be many souls whom grace is drawing to the prayer of simplicity but who are so cluttered up with considerations that they never come to it. It is like trying to push an overloaded Christmas tree through the narrow opening of the Bethlehem cave.

48

True piety knows its place, and is ready to stand aside with its armful of devotions when the soul is given the grace to pray in spirit and in truth. It is only false piety, or piety that is born of fear and not of love, which advances reasons for entertaining the prayer with rich variety. 'Aren't you afraid of doing nothing then?' asks false piety, 'surely you must know that generosity expresses itself in every way it can—all the time and without stop.'

So it is a good thing to take stock occasionally, and to assess the value of our pet practices in terms of the love of God. If the kingdom of God is not in meat and drink, nor is it in this or that devotion. Whatever certain authors claim, moved by what was undoubtedly a genuine light for *them,* the salvation of the generality of mankind will not depend upon the recitation of certain prayers, the wearing of certain scapulars, the observance of nine Fridays, the renunciation of personal merit in favour of the holy souls. These things may constitute a summons to some, but they do not amount to a general revelation.

The universal revelation is the summons to charity. This is something to which all of us must respond, and for the rest it is a matter of choice. The mature soul has sooner or later to distinguish between what is recommended as the result of an individual call and what is elicited in the name of faith. Faith, bypassing the totems of this or that devotional school, makes straight for the goal which is God.

49

The question arises as to how the simple prayer of faith relates to attendance at Mass. Does not the mind, when following the movement of the Mass, have to let go of this simplicity and take up a more diversified prayer? Admittedly the mind ranges over a number of subjects presented to it by what is going on at the altar, but its focus is still on God alone. The thought of God, and of union with him, holds the essential part of the soul while attention is given by the interior and exterior senses to the action of sacrifice.

In praying with Christ at the Mass we are not complicating our prayer but in fact are simplifying it. If Christ's prayer is unified, and if we share that prayer, our prayer too is unified. His is direct, immediate, simple, as he offers himself to the Father in sacrifice. So can ours be. The senses perceive in diversity, but the soul itself receives and responds in unity.

This is not an academic but a practical matter. In the history of Catholic spirituality the idea has been put forward that interior prayer is something so still and secret as to be incompatible with the act of assisting at Mass. The Mass would disturb the soul's tranquillity. The Mass is one kind of prayer (so the argument runs) and the silent search after God in the heart is another. The implication is that the soul has to come down from the mountain in order to witness the sacrifice in the plain. Since the sacrifice is Christ's, and since but for Christ's sacrifice we Christians could not pray at all, such a theory is surely inadmissible.

50

The more we understand about how we come to share in Christ's sacrifice, whether considered as Calvary or as the Mass, the richer our opportunity is seen to be. Familiarity with the idea of sharing in Christ's life should extend to the idea of sharing in his death. In the case of the saints the familiarity is such that the two ideas fuse into one and become habitual. For most of us the problem is not that of doctrine but of imagination: we cannot picture ourselves as having a part in either Christ's life or death.

'It is Christ who lives in me . . . my life is lived by faith in the Son of God . . . with Christ I am nailed to the cross . . . my life is hidden with Christ in God.' In making these statements St Paul was not implying that his life was something added to the life of Christ: rather he was claiming that Christ, taking the initiative, had identified himself, in death as in life, with his, Paul's, personality.

Our Lord had already taught that it was he who first chose us before we could think of choosing him. We add nothing to him; he adds everything to us. If we think of it in terms of time, the sequence could be put thus: he chooses us and gives himself to us; we receive him and he then expresses himself through us for our sanctification. Our true liberty and maturity lie in allowing full play to Christ acting by means of us. His life communicates itself not only to us but through us.

51

It is not enough to study the person, Christ, and then to imitate him. It is not a matter of impersonation but of participation. The closest impersonation would not get us very far. Impersonation assumes two separate activities: the activity of one identity is measured against the activity of another. But relationship with Christ supposes something much closer than this. Christ takes us up into his life—he whose identity it is to be Son of God—and we share his wholeness.

Taking his own illustration, namely the vine, we can develop the theme. Baptised Christians grow up in Christ from whom they derive their life. Because he is divine, Christ does not grow as a separate plant. Because he is human as well as divine, he grows as the stem of which we are branches. 'Dwell in me as I in you . . . apart from me you can do nothing.'

Cut a bunch of grapes off the vine, and what happens? For a while the grapes remain close to one another, and there may be nothing to show that they are separated from the stem. But they have lost the principle of their growth. As fruit they are already on the decline. Souls who cut themselves off from the principle of their lives, namely Christ, may be socially no different from what they were before. But there is now no fruit. Spiritually they are dead.

52

Our relationship with God can be seen under two aspects: as sons in relation to the Father and as sons in relation to Christ. Christ is the Son of the Father by nature, by the divine nature which he shares with the Father, whereas we are sons by adoption. Grace, through the merits of Christ, makes us sons. We do not have to pretend we are sons: we are made so in Christ.

If our human nature is incorporated into Christ's nature, and if he is the Son of God, we too must be sons of God. This sonship of ours, which we must get clear if we are to see how we share in Christ's sacrifice and prayer generally, is not something figurative. It is absolutely real. People are apt to think of this father-and-son relationship with God as fictional. Or at best as symbolic. Though it has to be taught in terms of natural paternity and sonship to make it intelligible at all, the concept points to more than a mere parallel.

In a human family an adopted son is related in all but the circumstance of natural birth. He is a member of the household, with legal rights and under obligations to behave in a particular way. 'God sent his Son that we might receive adoption . . . and if sons, heirs also through God's grace.' Because God has given himself to us in the person of his Son, who shares both the Father's nature and ours, we are made capable of sharing the 'fulness of Christ' which entitles us to call upon God as 'Abba, Father'. There is nothing metaphorical about this: it is an accurate appellation.

53

In addition to the privileges attaching to adoption there is the responsibility of acting in a way that the natural children of the family would act. As a consequence of our incorporation in Christ, we have the responsibility of acting as Christ acts— of living the life of the Son whose nature, besides being ours, is that of his Father.

Back now to the vine. For the branches to function as branches and not mere appendages, the connection with the parent stem has to be structural and organic. The branches belong to the vine, and the vine belongs to the branches. The whole Christ communicates himself to his brethren, to the branches of his own vine, whom he represents before the throne of his Father. They for their part are, in their response to grace, raised to a supernatural level. They too communicate, and what they communicate is Christ who is in them and by whose life they live.

So it is that, however weak and imperfect we are, we can find our place in Christ's sacrifice on Calvary and in the Mass.

Through no merit of ours but in virtue of our functional union with Christ as baptised Christians, we participate in the work of Christ as well as in his life. Accordingly we have a share in his prayer, in his sufferings, in his love . . . as we hope ultimately to have a share in his glory.

54

Man's finite endeavour is, in the grace which comes to us from the life and death of Christ, translated into infinite terms. For Christians to pray independently of the prayer of Christ would be more than a mere anomaly. It would be an impossibility. If Christ's help is needed for the performance of ordinary acts, it is needed all the more for the performance of specific acts of grace. Prayer, even non-mystical prayer, is a supernatural act: it cannot be done by nature alone. Prayer is strictly a work of grace.

This should explode the fallacy that attendance at Mass is an interruption of prayer. It is not even a lowering of the prayer of faith to a more elementary level. Union with Christ in his sacrificial act can hardly be a downgrading. The prayer of faith finds its destination in just such a union.

It is difficult to see how any personal prayer can rise above the condition of prayer to be found in the Mass. Since Christ's sacrifice assumes the plenitude of worship, and since man may share the act with him, the Mass, far from occasioning a loss to interior prayer, enriches recollection with the graces which flow from Calvary.

55

To some the idea of 'the liturgy', denoting complicated ritual, is distasteful. But understood in the light of the encyclical *Mediator Dei* liturgical worship finds its perfection not in ceremonial or a particular form of chant but in contemplation. After saying that the liturgy is 'public worship offered by Christ, head and members' the encyclical goes on to show that it is not a system imposed from without but is the prayer which emerges from a given structure. 'The liturgy is the life of faith, begun in baptism . . . and finding its fullest expression in contemplation.'

So the soul is initiated into the liturgical life when initiated into the life of Christ. Moreover the emphasis is seen to be on faith rather than on rites and observances. This should be reassuring to those who associate the liturgy with a particular culture. To possess the liturgical spirit it is not necessary to join an esoteric group or feel aesthetically moved. All that is needed to start with is faith, and this comes with baptism.

So it depends in practice upon what is made of the initial incorporation in Christ. It may show itself in this or that outward expression, but essentially the liturgy is interior worship held in common. It is the faith of the mystical body rendered to God in prayer. Corporate love, head and members, must find outlet, and this is the natural way for it to express itself.

56

Souls who are granted to pray in simplicity and faith find no division between attending to the Mass and attending to the single idea of God. Where love is the single principle there is little difference between any one prayer activity and any other. External worship fits into the scheme of the interior life, and the interior life adapts itself and expresses itself quite naturally in exterior worship. The principle of the liturgy, at the heart of which is sacrifice, is nothing more nor less than the principle of charity.

This may be all very well for the liturgy, but how do we square the interior exercise, which is more or less contemplative, with the practice of devotions? Do the stations of the cross, rosaries, novenas and so on interfere with the prayer of faith? Would it be wrong to speed up the silent waiting upon God with some hot-line invocations to the saints?

Once again the answer to these questions has to be particular rather than general. Each soul must respond to what is believed to be, for that individual soul, the grace of the moment. So long as it is a response and not a forcing, the exercise which attracts will prove no obstacle to interior prayer but will in fact help it. It would be illogical to exclude from the expression of love such exercises as are prompted by love. It is only when devotions are prompted by scruple or restlessness that they interrupt the interior exercise.

57

While praying wordlessly and in simplicity, a soul may be moved to express devotion to our Lady. Why suppress it? Our Lord must often have felt the same. Many who are in the way of faith like to make the stations of the cross every day; many resolve to recite a daily rosary. Why not? There were special prayers which devout Jews were urged to say each day, so presumably the holy family said them. Did Jesus, Mary, and Joseph suffer loss to their contemplation by conforming to popular devotion?

Only when fear is the dominant motive do devotions cease to devotions—acts, that is, of loving piety—and become obsessive compulsions. Souls who seriously practice prayer come to distinguish between what is undertaken to please God and what is undertaken as a sop to self. They will also be able to preserve a balance in their religious exercises, not attaching more importance to devotions than to interior prayer or to prayers of obligation.

Resolutions to do this or that every day for the love of God possess one disadvantage: the love of God can all too soon be replaced by the fear of not keeping the resolution. The discipline imposed may be good for the character, the actual exercise may be good in itself, the intention may be good as first conceived, but once fear has cast out love there is not much point in going on with it.

58

Fortunately love has more power to cast out fear than fear has power to cast out love. So it should not be too difficult to change an imperfect motive into a better one. When we catch ourselves acting from fear, from routine, from human respect, or even from motives which are downright wrong, we can redirect and purify until the act, now performed in Christ, is one of high perfection.

A virtuous act is one done in charity, in Christ. Love is accordingly the prime consideration. Given love as the source and the end of a course of action, it is a mistake to examine too closely the subsidiary motives. Secondary motives, since they can materially influence the action, are important; but they are not so important that their examination becomes a nightmare. Good actions can be paralysed by the anxiety to know their origins. If we are clear about the destination, we can afford to forget about the original impulse.

While we have every reason to suspect our hidden motives we have no excuse for making a morbid study of them. It is better to commit them in a general way to God and to concentrate on steering the work by the light of his love. Consciousness of self-interest does not prevent our loving God whereas preoccupation with self-interest very well might.

59

Knowing that in his dealings with us God has no other motive than love, we for our part have to try to match this disposition. With the saints, love is the sole impulse. When St Francis of Sales was asked whether it was more perfect to pick a flower or leave it growing, he said: 'Do either—it doesn't matter which—but do it for the love of God.' The kingdom of heaven is not in details of meat and drinik, but even meat and drink become sanctified when the love of God is brought to bear upon them.

The attitude of mind which refers the commonplace events of every day to God is not arrived at all at once. It develops as the prayer of faith develops. Indeed it is one of the effects of this prayer. As life tends towards simplicity and trust, the network of motives ceases to disturb. Where love is the criterion there is no longer the tension of fear. Fear makes a superstition of what was designed to promote love but has never been given a chance to practice it. The prayer of faith shows up all this.

'For the unity of two entities,' says St Bernard, 'there must be correspondence of terms.' Since there is no fear in God, it must be on a basis of love that the human entity unites with the divine. In the sense that our fears can be united with the human fear of Christ there is a connection, but even here the union is one of love and not of fear. Fear is useful as a trial—it is the most searching of all trials—and therefore as an incentive to the act of trust, but not for much else. Certainly the sooner it gives way to love the better.

60

The simplicity of approach which is brought to bear upon the liturgy is extended towards the Church. Once the soul is settled in the way of faith, which is a prayer condition and not a question of natural choice, the demands of the Church are seen in unity rather than in diversity. The Church is seen not as a legislative body, not as an heirarchical system, not even as an infallible authority. It is seen as Christ. Just as Christ's human nature disguised his divine nature, so the Church's beurocratical structure disguises its Christological authenticity.

The Church provides us with the means by which the faithful, members of Christ's mystical body, express Christ's life. In giving us the sacraments, the Church enables us to identify ourselves with the various activities of Christ, enables us to make Christ's works our own. The life and merits of Christ—otherwise, to borrow from the terminology of finance, frozen—become by the Church's prerogative available to man. Whatever Christ's representatives bind on earth is bound also in heaven, whatever they loose on earth is loosed also in heaven.

Prayer sees all this without argument or question. Faith transcends—may even, if it is imperfect, be too eager to transcend—the clauses of the discussion. This is perhaps the only drawback to simplicity: it over-simplifies. But at least it is better than multiplying difficulties.

61

To those outside the Church, or even to those who belong to the Church but who do not pray, the idea of the mystical body must savour of pious fiction. How can the faithful, most of whom are unfaithful, be an extension of Christ? How can the members claim to be in organic relationship with the head, Christ? How can we be said, in any real way, to continue or 're-live' Christ's life?

This is where faith in the Church comes in. Without the Church to give it to us, the sharing of Christ's life would be unattainable. All we would have to go on would be the text of the gospel, and there would be no certainty that even this was divinely inspired. As it is we have the Church telling us of our place in Christ's life, of what we have to do to develop this relationship, and of the absolute trust we can place in her teaching.

Truth is undivided. Once we acknowledge in the Church the same truth that we acknowledge in Christ, we can approach the whole of religion in simplicity. Christ, glorified in heaven, reveals himself in the Church and communicates himself through the Church. Hence the sacraments, hence infallible pronouncements, hence the Church's commandments. In assenting to the Church we assent to Christ, and if we want to grow in Christ we look to the Church to tell us how to.

62

Failure to identify Christ with his Church can explain how heresies, schisms, persecutions, ecclesistical anomalies and sectarian divisions have come about. This would be a question for the Church historian. More immediately it explains how individual souls can go against the mind of the Church while professing wholehearted devotion to the person of Christ. It explains but does not excuse. To the properly instructed, and still more to those seriously practising prayer, the mind of the Church reflects the mind of Christ.

Even if we miss the mind of Christ as reflected in the Church, we ought to be able to recognise it as revealed in the Church's sacraments. We should know not only what his intention was when he instituted the sacraments but what it is now when each sacrament is conferred upon each member of his Church.

Just as his miracles were manifestations of his love, power, and divine authority, so Christ's sacraments, dispensed by the Church, are manifestations of the same things. Each miracle was in this sense a revelation; each sacrament is in this sense a revelation. Miracles and sacraments are evidence of divine authority. The recognition of this divine authority at work in an outward form, and particularly when this authority is deputised down the heirarchical scale till it reaches the humblest human minister of the sacrament, is apt material for the exercise of faith. 'May our Lord Jesus Christ absolve you; and I with his authority do absolve you . . .'

63

The sacramental system, the authority vested in pope and bishops to define infallibly, the voice of scripture and tradition: these things are not just 'good medicine'. They are the means appointed by Christ whereby he imparts himself to the members of his Church for their sanctification. Each single individual is the object of their influence. None of these things would exist if the salvation of the human soul, the individual human soul, were not at stake. 'The sabbath was made for man, not for the sabbath.'

Though our faith in the truth of the Church is in exact ratio to our faith in the truth of God, we are not expected to give to the pronouncements of churchmen the credence which we give to the divine law. It would be a poor compliment to God and his Church if, in the name of humble obedience, we were to waive the examination of credentials. Laziness and the desire to feel secure in blind submission can be mistaken for true obedience and simple faith. Faith is not quite as simple as that, and for obedience to be true it does not have to be unthinking.

Many enter the religious life because they will not have to think thereafter. They will be able to shut their minds, and simply do what they are told. Such an arrangement they imagine to be the height of virtue. But what sort of service is that? How can love express itself in a mechanical repetition of routines? What is so wrong about the human intellect, God's greatest natural gift to man, that it must be muzzled if religion is to be practised in full perfection?

64

Wholesale religious assumptions are not the same as acts of faith, and it may well be the Christian's duty to find reasonable backing for some of the things which it would be much easier to take on faith. Beyond a certain point to 'take on faith' is a sign of irresponsibility.

A man may justify his assumptions by appealing to his innate feeling for truth. What is the difference between this and intuition? The Church is shy of intuition. Intuition is not safe enough to be trusted on matters of faith. The Church prefers reason. The unforgiveable sin is based upon an uncritical assumption, upon an irresponsible intuition.

'So the Church prefers *reason*,' retorts the man of so-called faith, 'I thought what the Church wanted was blind obedience.' Obedience, yes, but not blindfolded. If faith is to be what it is meant to be, if the service of God is to be a 'reasonable service', there must sooner or later be a confrontation with the forces opposed to faith. It is one of the curious paradoxes of the spiritual life that those who are most against reason and in favour of faith are just those who are guilty of rationalisation. They rationalise submission.

65

There is no merit in making a fetish of faith, whereby the more unlikely a thing is the more merit there is in believing it. Trust in the Church's guidance does not entitle the faithful to submerge themselves under the comprehensive cover of orthodoxy, confident that the Church can be left to do all the deciding for them. While it is true that the Church serves its members —just as Christ came 'not to be ministered to but to minister' —it is not a substitute for the members' service. And service means choice, decision, reflection, and repeated choice.

The Church of Christ is a servant church, not a master church. It does not hand out cotton-wool which the faithful obediently pull over their eyes. The faithful are as much the Church as the ecclesiastical leaders are the Church. One of the major benefits to come out of the Second Vatican Council is the place in the Church given to the layman. The implications of this are numerous, not the least of them being the layman's responsibility, shared with the clergy, of thinking.

If in the last analysis religion is a person-to-person relationship, the soul has to act as a person. Since Christ does not look upon the members of his Church as pieces on a board, the members themselves may not act as though they held this view. The Christian's duty goes beyond acceptance of the Christian claim. With its sacraments and doctrines the Church provides the means, but in making use of the means the Christian has still to exercise his inalienable powers as man. He has to pass judgment, determine his course, continue to justify his freedom of will.

66

Parents, religious superiors, ecclesiastical authorities—all in fact who have the right to command—can make automatons of their subjects. By denying a subject responsibility, the superior may get an unthinking obedience, which is perhaps immediately convenient, but it is a shortsighted policy to pursue: love cannot grow out of it, because love supposes thought. What is likely to grow out of it is either fear, rebellion, or apathy.

The value of submission lies in the renunciation of a right, the right to independence. Renunciation for the love of God, and not from dread of the consequences or for peace at the price of surrender. A man's left hand would not serve the body by going numb and allowing itself to be pushed about like a piece of wood by the right hand.

It is chiefly by prayer that souls learn how to balance these questions of independence, responsibility, renunciation, obedience. Prayer shows us how far we are to go in identifying ourselves with the society to which we belong while at the same time retaining the identity which God means us to have. Always we are persons in Christ, not units surrendered either to personal expedience or to the more altruistic idea of collective therapy. We are made, each one of us uniquely, in the image and likeness of God.

67

Spiritual maturity, which is what personal responsibility in religion amounts to, does not take away from obedience but on the contrary adds to it. By seeing all round the question it can render a more enlightened submission. Prayer opens up new possibilities of self-renunciation so that whatever the judgment formed about the command, or about the authority commanding it, the surrender of the will is increasingly purified.

Though the order given may appear injudicious, and the superior ill-informed or prejudiced or plain stupid, the course is clear. If obedience against such odds is practised in secular services, it ought to be all the more possible to practise it in a service which in any case is one of faith. Prayer so sharpens

47

and extends faith that the soul, whether vowed to it or not, comes to live by obedience. Without sacrificing anything of his uniqueness as a person, a man chooses to follow other people's wishes in preference to his own.

It is a question of trust. Believing in the providence of God, a man is led by his prayer to see in situations created by other people expressions of this providence. He accepts both the occasions and the perpetrators of the occasions in the spirit of submission. He is obedient. He does not have to pretend that wisdom and justice have prevailed in the world around him. He is probably more conscious than most of the travesties which beset human affairs. But this is not his concern. His concern is to trust in the providence of God and surrender himself to it.

68

To trust in the hour-to-hour providential will of God is virtually to pray without ceasing. Moreover the scope of this trust is extended according to the soul's response to grace during actual prayer time. The soul comes to think of trust not so much as a knack of the mind which dismisses the possibility of foregoing the reward promised to trust, but rather as that kind of confidence which no amount of foregoing will disturb.

'The faith which moves mountains' is understood not in its obvious meaning—namely that if you *really* believe, if you can work yourself into the state of mind which has no doubts at all, you will be able to see the miracle worked before your very eyes—but rather in the more subtle sense of discovering, as the result of perseverance in faith, that what had seemed like mountainous obstacles were in fact no obstacles at all: God has moved them.

Souls of faith are not greatly bothered by mountains. They know that God will either take them away or else give the grace to climb over them. Those who get high enough above the world can view the land beneath them in simplicity. Only when they are on a level with the line of vision do mountains loom large and block the way. When the level of vision is raised above them, the obstacles are seen to be less menacing. Trust may not eliminate all obstacles, and prayer may not solve all problems, but with faith and prayer the soul is at least equipped to meet all needs.

69

St John's fourteenth chapter opens with our Lord's words: 'Let not your hearts be troubled. Trust in God always; trust also in me.' Twelve verses further on we have our Lord giving the consequences of this trust: 'Amen, amen, I say to you, he who has faith in me will do those things which I do . . . indeed whatever you ask in my name I will do, so that the Father may be glorified in the Son.'

We read these texts, and at once, as in the matter of moving mountains into the sea, we grope about for the right act of faith. Shall we never discover the magic phrase which will release so much divine force and produce for us such enviable results? Once again we are seeing the question of trust from the wrong angle, from our own angle rather than from God's.

Surely these injunctions and promises cannot mean that when the temperature of our faith has risen to a certain degree we shall succeed in performing the kind of works which in the gospels we see Christ performing. Surely it is not a matter of pressing the gift of faith to a pitch of intensity *or* of reproducing particular acts. More in keeping with our Lord's teaching, and St Paul's, would be to suppose him as saying: 'I trust the Father in all things, and as a result I glorify him in all things . . . he hears me by arranging my life and setting his seal to my works . . . if you trust him as I do, he will do the same for you . . . you will be leading my life . . . ask for this and see . . . instead of being broken by the world you will find yourself transcending the world . . . you will be giving glory to the Father and to me . . . so have faith.'

70

If I could look at my life from God's point of view I would be less confused when I see it failing to give me the kind of happiness I expect from it. I would also be less confused when, having applied the gospel remedies of prayer and trust, I am no better off. The key has opened nothing after all. The fault lies in my impatience, greed, false standards of valuation.

As seen by God, my life, since it is Christ's life lived in me, is justified. The prayer and trust to which, however badly

I practise them, I am committed, have in fact been verified. I have prayed in Christ's name, believing as best I could, and God has given me himself. 'Then you will know that I am in the Father, and you in me and I in you . . . he who loves me will be loved by my Father.'

The texts which promise me so much do not have to be watered down to suit my disappointment: they have to be read as if with the mind which inspired them. When God has given me his life and his love, I cannot complain that I have been cheated of that for which I asked in his name. The significant thing is not my little happiness as I see it, foreshortened and unrelated to anything apart from myself, but my capacity for infinite happiness which is seen and provided for by God. How does God view this thing which I ask for so hungrily in Christ's name, and which I am sure will substantially affect my happiness? Does he judge it to be more important than his own life which he is giving me?

71

If when we speak of prayer and faith *transcending* the drawbacks to human existence we mean a blind uncaring ascent into a dream world where the realities of life are left behind for others to cope with, we have got it wrong. Nor should we think of that true mystical state in which the intellect and will are temporarily held captive in the soul's union with God so that outward affairs are not observed. 'Transcendence' here denotes neither an escape assisted by the imagination nor a suspension which is of grace, but rather the detachment which is brought about by the spirit but which has not lost touch with the things of sense.

Without suppressing the emotions, faith enables the soul to rise above the emotions. And if this sounds cold and superior, it must be remembered that those who are essentially souls of faith, the saints, are just those who feel things deeply. It is because they feel things deeply that they are able to help others, and again it is because they feel things deeply that their prayer is all the more pleasing to God.

So to transcend the contingencies of life is not the same as to hold aloof, to show indifference, to avoid involvement. Anything which breeds insensitivity is bound to be on the wrong lines. Compassion, as we know from the example of Christ and his mother, is inherent in the service of God. Followers of Christ must necessarily be involved. It is their vocation to live as members of one another. But by their faith and prayer they will use material contacts as a lever to the world of the spirit. Involvement, instead of pulling them down from the contemplation of God, will raise their natural operation, because performed in charity, to the supernatural level. To transcend is properly to translate.

72

Souls of prayer have as many difficulties as other people, probably more, but in faith they pray through them. They still get doubts, they still feel badly about themselves and their past, they still have their spasms of fear, loneliness, resentment against the circumstances of life and the waste; they still find themselves wishing they had decided differently and that the future were not so bleak. But despite all this they refuse, in the will, to be disappointed. Save in the matter of sin, they have no regrets.

The combination of prayer and faith, then, is a liberating force which no human wretchedness has power to restrain. Forces which spring from natural character are limited in their range: idealism may free a man from cynicism, humanity from hardness of heart, generosity from meanness, and so on. The influence exercised by faith and prayer is without limit. This is because God is its source.

Not only is despair ruled out for the soul of faith but the bitterness which leads on to despair. Even self-pity, the natural disposition for bitterness, is exposed and brushed aside. Whatever the frustrations, interior and exterior, the soul of faith meets every fluctuation in the spirit of hope. Indeed if hope is not the outcome—a hope which can take failure and injustice and the hazards of the future in its stride—there is something wrong with the soul's prayer.

73

In the case of the saints the will of God is paramount, and according to how it affects God's will every temporal importance drops into place. Consequently there is order in the soul, and to a large extent also in the handling of outward affairs. This does not mean that the saint is necessarily granted the light to see the relative significance of the steps he takes, but at least it ensures the overall significance. Neither faith nor prayer guarantee sound judgment, and if they do not render the soul proof against mistakes, they do at least, if maintained conscientiously, guard against malice. Love is the standard, the bar to which decisions are referred.

It is one of the tragedies of sin that, if obstinately persevered in, the area of error is enlarged. The sinner is so used to choosing selfishly that love is no longer seen as the only touchstone of any value. The outlines of right and wrong become blurred, and it becomes in the sinner's interest to keep them so. In the false light of sin it is easy to label evil as good and good as evil, and this, as Isaias says, is the ultimate apostacy.

When the soul prefers blindness to vision there is nothing for the light of grace to work on. Lacking the light to which the baptised soul has a right, it is easy for the sinner to become an agnostic. It is not that he chooses agnosticism as an escape and an excuse (though this may be the case too) but that by consistently sinning against the light he now lacks the light to be a believer.

74

So long as he leaves his soul open to grace, even if he does not pray for it or think about it, the sinner stands a good chance. He has not chosen evil as the environment to which he belongs; he virtually admits that there might conceivably be a change. In the accepted sense he may have lost his faith. He may be placing his hope in the wrong things or in nothing at all. He may have mistaken the nature of love and turned it inside out. But the fact that he would still accept truth if he saw it, even if he does not know he would, is from God's point of view disposition enough. Strictly the man may not deserve grace, light, mercy: he has put himself beyond the normal reach of these things. But then which of us deserves them anyway?

Living with sin as one's habitual state is like living underground: it is possible, but not what man is born to. Man's proper element is light, not darkness. When constantly in darkness, his sight eventually fails so that he does not recognise the light when it is presented to him. If he wants to see again he must come up from underground and accustom himself to living in the light. The perspectives can return to him, but he has to make the effort. And some of the things which he sees about himself may make him wish that he was back in his darkness, because blindness can be more comfortable than self-knowledge.

Most of us are neither out-and-out sinners nor out-and-out saints; we live in an uncommitted area in between. For us consequently the terms of God's will are never crystal clear, and we are never absolutely sure that we know what he wants. But then if we were absolutely sure where would be the faith? Where would be the search which is the point of it all? Where would be the dependence upon God which is conditioned by never being absolutely certain about anything?

75

In the parable of the wheat and cockle, a point which is frequently missed is that wheat and cockle look very much alike. If cockle resembled brambles or thistles or holly, there would be more of a case for picking out an obviously different plant from wheat. But cockle is simply alien corn, something so like the real thing as to be indistinguishable at the first growth. 'By their fruits you shall know them.' The good corn grows to be harvested and to be put to the service of man, the bad corn shows its quality when it winds itself round the stalks of the good and stifles its growth.

Often we cannot distinguish between God's will and our own, between altruistic and selfish desires, between true and false religious spirit, between faith and fatalism, between the service of God and personal ambition. The world is full of things which look true but are false. And there are even a few things which look false but turn out to be true. How do we know that everything is not an illusion? We cannot be as sure as would like to be about God, the Church, life after death, the validity of scripture, so how can we be sure of those things which they give rise to? Yet if we were perfectly sure, and if there were no fear of delusion, where would be the faith?

If human existence could be explained, and all its mysteries solved, there would be too little to work for to make it interesting. It is the contradictions which make us look for truth; it is the unfairness which makes us plan for justice; it is the cruelty and disloyalty and fickleness and worldly cynicism which makes the ideal of love worth holding. And then as regards God, there has to be about him that which man's mind cannot grasp. If God were known to our human intelligence in such a way that we could comprehend him—that is, fully take him in—he would be subject to us. We cannot expect to understand him as he understands us.

76ᐧ

The creator comprehends his creatures not only because he is omniscient but because he has designed created natures as knowable. Had man created animals he would be able to comprehend them. As it is he knows relatively little about animals, other human beings, God. What knowledge he has is the gift of God, who alone possesses wisdom in its fulness, and who deals out knowledge to his creatures according to his providential will. It is not our knowledge—whether in relation to God, to one another, or to the natural order—which is the ground of our faith. Indeed it is our lack of knowledge which makes faith all the more necessary to us.

Knowledge, like love, must be active. The reasoning mind must increase its knowledge, taking it step by step and from truth to truth, in the direction of wisdom itself which is absolute truth. Unfortunately most of us are only too ready to stop long short of the knowledge which we could possess if we worked harder for it. While knowledge is not in this life the end, it is, when supplemented by faith, a great help towards sanctification.

Faith is more important than knowledge, because while it is impossible for man to know all truth it is possible for him to believe in all truth. Faith takes over where knowledge ceases, carrying the soul past proof and the lack of proof, past reliance on another's word, past intuition and hesitation, past the need of all assurance save that of faith itself.

77

It might be argued that the hazards of faith outweigh its

blessings. If it is possible to believe in the wrong teaching, to see truth where there is no truth, not to see truth where there is truth, and to rebel instinctively against the right teaching, would it not be simpler to forget about the theological side of religion and concentrate on loving one's neighbour? Love after all is the main thing, and if one gets that right why bother about the rest?

There are many who believe in an after-life because they cannot imagine temporal existence to be worth while without it. In the same way they can believe in the existence of God because they cannot imagine how anyone except a creator can benefit by creation. But this is about the sum of their creed. They see no reason why they should have to accept the Trinity, an infallible Church, dogmas, sacraments, and the rest. 'Whether he was divine or not,' they say of our Lord, 'he taught the universal obligation of love, and that's quite enough for me . . . you can keep your services and saints.'

Such a line of reasoning is so common that we need to see clearly where the fallacy lies. All right: charity. Of course charity is the most important thing, but the point is that you cannot isolate charity. You cannot practise it unrelated to obedience, humility, trust, hope, justice and so on. Charity is the 'bond of perfection', binding all the other virtues together: it is not the rubber stamp which dispenses from the practice of the other virtues. Once admit charity into your soul and you find you have to follow it up with obedience, humility, trust, hope, justice and so on.

78

Charity expands, opens up new possibilities at every turn. It may begin with a purely humanitarian service of others but it will develop, if it is genuinely open hearted and open minded, into some sort of service of God. The man who loves in the spirit of Christ will find it impossible to evade the question of Christ's divinity. Accepting Christ's divinity, he will want to examine the implications of Christ's teaching on charity. He will see that he must pray. An effect of his prayer will be the granting of light, and light will reveal the existence of the Trinity, the necessity of an infallible Church, the place in the Christian scheme of dogmas, sacraments, saints, services and the rest.

People talk about being fundamentalists, about taking their stand on religious essentials, but you cannot be a fundamentalist without accepting what the foundations are there to support. Admittedly there can be exaggeration in the superstructure, but you cannot have a building composed solely of foundations.

79

Benevolence without the grace of charity tends to become either bureaucratic or sentimental. It is not easy to keep one's human relationships at a supernatural level, for without prayer and faith they fall naturally into one or other pattern set by the world. The social life which does not take its character from the spiritual life takes its character from the environment in which its operates.

To the man of prayer and faith, to the complete Christian, society is nothing else than the mystical body of Christ. He knows that his friends, and the men and women among whom he works, are not of his choosing but of God's. He has been placed among them not so that he may enjoy them but so that he may serve them. Not for their company but for their use in bringing them and him nearer to God. Friendship is either a luxury, a means of gratifying self, or a gift from God which is meant to be used in the service of God.

Many would say that in working for the salvation of others it is enough to meet them on a purely natural level, and be oneself. But does not charity mean more than this? The whole point about the Christian apostolate is that it is *not* something purely natural. Applied negatively, the be-yourself-and-make-frietnds-with-them theory would justify a man's withdrawing from his social circle when it suited him. The man who is moved by charity, who has a genuine zeal for souls, knows that it is just when he is bored by other people that he must stop on among them. It is the man who is moved by his moods who treats the company of others as though it existed for his entertainment. The man of charity knows that his circle has been formed by God.

80

If many interpret charity too loosely, seeing in it no more

than natural fellowship, there are many who interpret it just as loosely by seeing it as the performance of a duty. St Augustine's statement already quoted in relation to the love of God ('the duty of loving God is not fulfilled when it is performed as a duty') might equally apply in relation to the love of neighbour. Certainly for the perfection of Christian charity we are expected to do more than merely satisfy an obligation.

The apostle has not finished when he has delivered his message, the parent has not finished when the children are fed and clothed, the priest has not finished when he has left the altar and the confessional. Christians, lay as well as professional, are asked to carry Christ to the souls of their fellow men. In order that this may be effective, God gives to each the grace to go beyond charity's immediate obligation. It requires faith to see this, and still more faith to put it in practice.

It is one of the universal laws of the spiritual life that those who live in closest union with God are those who do most in the service of other people. This is because in faith and charity they make for the important qualities in human relationship, and leave aside the superficialities which are thought to be significant by worldly people. The essential bond must be Christ, and the affinity which we bear to one another must be seen in our common likeness to Christ.

81

If charity to others were made the basis of our decisions, we might have to put up with a lot of inconvenieince but we would benefit in a number of unexpected ways. The greatest inconvenience to devout people would be having to reduce their religious practices in order to make room for undertakings of charity. In this they feel they are withdrawing from the absolute good and attending to a relative good. They are leaving the certain for the questionable. But what if the absolute and certain good, God, prefers it this way?

Theologians distinguish between affective and effective charity. Charity is affective when the soul renders the love of God directly to God in prayer; it is effective when it works indirectly through the necessity of the moment. So there is no loss to the essential of charity when a person has to tear himself away from his interior exercises at the call of exterior duty. He must take it with the readiness which Mary would have shown had our Lord told her to go and help Martha with the dishes.

This principle of leaving the presence of God in prayer to find the presence of God in the existing need is easier to put into operation if we ask ourselves what it is that God really wants of us. Our prayer or our surrender? Having given the obvious answer to the question, we can see the necessary place of obedience in the spiritual life. Without obedience there can be no surrender, and without surrender the life of prayer is incomplete. It was because his love for the Father and for man caused him to lay down his life in witness to charity that it could be said of Christ: 'He was obedient unto death, even to the death of the cross.'

82

Charity and obedience: these are the aspects to consider in any given situation when deciding what course to follow. It is not easy to brush aside the other elements which enter in— such as the hardship involved, the cost, the effect on health or sleep or nerves, the prospect of failure—but this is just where faith comes in. Trust can operate on just this sort of material.

Even with such a simple guide to go by—how does it look, up against love and obedience?—complications abound. Charity can wriggle out from under the weight of the law, and the law can be called in to ride roughshod over charity. A religious dispenses himself from the rule of silence in order, out of charity, to gossip; a layman stays away from Mass so as not to offend a guest; a parent, out of love, neglects to correct a son or daughter for breaking a commandment.

If glaring misconceptions can flourish in the name of charity, the same may be said regarding obedience. Here are two examples which happen to be true. In 1945 some four tons of high explosive were entrusted to an officer of the British Home Guard who was instructed to conceal the material in his garden, to maintain absolute secrecy, and to await further orders. In 1964, nineteen years later, the oversight was discovered and the bombs, gelignite, and grenades—by now in a highly dangerous condition—were immunized. The officer was obedient, but what about charity?

In a French convent a postulant upset a bottle of ink on the floor of her cell, and, not knowing where the mops and cloths were kept, sought help from the first sister she came across. The sister, putting her finger to her lip, went off to look for a superior who could give her permission to enter another's cell and break silence. She returned to find the postulant in tears and the ink soaked indelibly into the bare boards.

In both the cases cited above, where the letter stifled the spirit, common sense would have helped. Common sense does not necessarily rationalise virtue, much less go against it. Common sense more often coincides with charity than contradicts it.

83

Residing in the practical intellect, common sense is no substitute for grace, but can be a good foundation for faith and prayer. Certainly a lot more faith and prayer would be needed to make good the deficiency if it were lacking. People who regard themselves as natural mystics are far less likely to become supernatural mystics than those who are straightforward realists with no pretensions.

The man who relies on intuition rather than horse sense lays himself open to delusion. Faith and the habit of prayer are not as invulnerable as might be imagined: they need to be backed by a calm dependence not only upon God but upon fact. Not everyone can count upon possessing a sound practical judgment, but everyone can adopt a humble attitude towards the working of grace in his soul. To search in simplicity after truth—sheer matter-of-fact truth which is God himself—is more humble than to sit about waiting for a mystical experience.

As a corollary it might be added that in the instruction of children on spiritual matters, it is important to avoid the suggestion of magic. Nothing can be so misleading as the idea that God is forever breaking his natural law to satisfy his supernatural one. Miracles, sure enough, are not only possible but may be prayed for without scruple, but at the same time the normal way for God to work, so the Church teaches, is through the natural order. Though a miracle is in no sense a violation, it is a suspension of the natural law.

84

It is all very well to talk of applying the test of, jointly, charity and obedience to our undertakings but, even so, how do we know that self-interest is not really at the back of it all the time? For example, having pretended to ourselves that our motives are upright, we can drag in charity and obedience as afterthoughts. We can so manoeuvre the situation as to win tributes to our kindness of heart while superiors find themselves directing us to do what we have decided to do in any case.

The charity test must show that we are working from the inside, and are not treating it merely as an excuse, as a voucher to be stuck on. The obedience test must, in the same way, show where the project is starting from, and not use the permission as a reassurance in an evasion. If charity to one's neighbour begins with consideration for people's feelings, and if obedience to authority begins with anticipating a superior's wishes, it can be seen how both virtues lead away from self and into the needs of others. They rule out personal ambition, envy, meanness, arrogance.

A point to be stressed here is that all Christian virtues, and this is especially true of charity and obedience, are essentially liberative. Observing the obligations they put upon us, we are tempted to think the opposite. Despite its manifold demands, charity is the freedom to love others in Christ. We are too ready to be wearied by the manifold demands, and not ready enough to acknowledge the freedom. It is the same with obedience: we remember the restraints and forget about what it releases us from. 'Where the spirit of the Lord is' says St Paul to the Corinthians, 'there is liberty.'

85

The notion of Christian freedom, attained to in Christ and expressed by love and submission, is strong in St Paul. To the Galatians he writes: 'Christ set us free . . . you were called to be free men, but do not turn your freedom into licence . . . but be servants to one another in love . . . if you are led by the spirit you are not under the law . . . the harvest of the spirit is love.' St Paul seems obsessed with man's need to understand the real significance of law, and not to let himself get so tied up in it that he will not be able to practise the love which makes him free.

'Bear one another's burdens,' is St Paul's conclusion of the subject in his letter to the Galatians, 'and in this way you will fulfil the law of Christ.' If only, we say, it could be as simple as that. Here we are with Canon Law (running to 2,414 paragraphs), with liturgical decrees (thousands of them, and constantly being added to), Conciliar pronouncements (at the time of writing not yet numbered), regional directories and diocesan instructions. In what way, we wonder, does all this make us *free?*

Rules, like dogmas, are designed to elicit a particular response. Neither rules nor dogmas are presented to us for our mortification but for the freedom which we shall enjoy when we come up with the required reaction. It all depends upon whether we approach them in humility and submission or with resentment and criticism. Given love, we can make the yoke of the law serve the spirit and freely express our faith in much the same way that prayer freely expresses our faith. Lacking love, we can allow rules to dwarf our minds, poison our prayer, restrict our liberty. 'Stand firm then' St Paul exhorts, 'and refuse to be tied to the yoke of slavery again.'

86

A fact which many can appreciate only when they are living in sin is that they would be far more free if they kept the rules. A canary might complain about the restrictions of its cage, but let it out in the open and you put it at the mercy of other birds. This idea of liberty under law is no fiction; without law you get licence, and licence is not at all the same thing as freedom. Obedience is subjection to a higher law; licence is subjection to a lower one. There is no slavery like that endured by the licentious.

But there is another and more immediately spiritual argument to justify the liberative nature of religious law: in subjecting ourselves to law we are uniting ourselves with the subjection of Christ; and Christ was free. We would be unlike Christ if we did not submit, freely, to authority. Just as Christ not only obeyed but also loved what the Father commanded, so we should obey and even try to love what is commanded by the Father and handed down to us through men. To reject, in a bid for liberty, what God has handed down in a bid for man's obedience is logically to reject Christ.

Before the conclusion is drawn from this that to oppose every man-made law, however trivial, is to oppose Christ a distinction must be made. But it is a distinction which cannot be made without the combined exercise of grace and common sense. A man's prayer will tell him how to use his practical judgment in discerning between a routine regulation and a directive which can be traced back ultimately to the Holy Spirit.

87

When I am instructed on an envelope to mail early for Christmas, do I, on pain of withdrawing by obedience from the obedience of Christ, have to comply? When the traffic light tells me to wait, am I offending God if I walk? When I am bidden fasten my seat-belt in a plane, must I regard this as an articulation of God's law? Not? Well, you see why it was necessary to drag in common sense.

If the matter is so easily solved by common sense, why drag in prayer and grace. The reason is not hard to find. *Without* prayer and grace to give it backing, common sense can become the cloak of false liberty. Even given the spiritual safeguards, there is no guarantee against mistakes. While it may not be difficult to judge the binding force of such keep-off-the-grass legislation as enumerated above, it becomes less clear when the man-made rules come from a religious and not a secular authority.

In the liturgical regulations for instance. *Must* I answer the responses aloud with everyone else, follow the directions about kneeling and standing and sitting, give up my private system of assisting at Mass? In questions of education, the family, race relations, social justice, do I *have* to bow to the current ecclesiastical view or may I have my own ideas? With regard to the first point, the answer depends upon what the questioner is aiming at, mediocrity or perfection. As for the second, it depends upon whether the moral law is involved in the particular question at issue.

88

In an audience on July 14th, 1965, Pope Paul spoke of the prevailing hostility to authority, secular and religious: 'Obedience—that is to say the welcoming and practical recognition of authority—is continually being questioned as being contrary to the development of the human person, as being unworthy of free, mature and adult human beings. There are those who think it worthwhile to run the risk of a liberating disobedience, and there is no lack of able people who delude themselves, maybe without saying it openly, that they can be excellent or at least sufficiently good Catholics while reserving for themselves an absolute autonomy of thought and action.'

If 'autonomy of thought and action' may be justified in the case of such liturgical regulations as are mentioned above (and this will be discussed later), it can never be justified where it is a question of the natural law. Here obedience to the Church's ruling as to what is and what is not the natural law must be absolute. But while we need neither an angel from heaven or a jurist from Rome to tell us that abortion is forbidden, we do need to be told how to think and what to do about discrimination (whether of race, class, or religion), the right to strike, birth-control, nuclear warfare and the position of the conscientious objector.

God is not the God of many laws, says Karl Rahner in his book *Encounters with Silence,* but of one law: One law that we should give our love and service to him alone. This covers the whole of our obedience, whether to temporal or spiritual authority. 'You would have no power over me,' said our Lord to Pilate, 'were it not granted you by my Father.' If we truly love Christ and his Father, we see in all authority the power of God. So shall we submit to the one law.

89

Considering now the other kind of legislation—lesser enactments promulgated by Rome or the local heirarchy—there is again a distinction. If it is made clear that the decree is binding under sin, the duty of the Catholic is obvious. Such would be the case in the condemnation of a play, film, or book; in the banning of certain drugs; in forbidding parents to send their children to non-Catholic schools; in regulations about fasting. Some things are forbidden because they are wrong (artificial insemination, driving at a speed that endangers life); others are wrong because they are forbidden (eating meat on Fridays, receiving Communion more than once in the day). The faithful have to abide, either way, by the Church's ruling.

Where the question of sin is not explicitly stated (vocal assistance at the dialogue Mass, the sum to be put in the plate, the dress to be worn in the *domaine* at Lourdes, participation in novenas, holy hours, processions, and in general complying with the innumerable recommendations which are made from the pulpit on Sundays) the faithful may use their discretion.

So much for the juridical aspect of the subject. But this is something different from the interior aspect. In the perfecting of obedience what we need chiefly to examine is not this or that category of law but rather the soul's personal response to law as a whole, to *the* law as reflecting the will of God. This brings us to a new dimension of obedience which simplifies matters greatly. 'Isaias was right,' said our Lord, 'when he said about you hypocrites, "these people pay me lip-service, but their heart is far from me for they teach as doctrines the commandments of men." You neglect the commandment of God in order to observe the tradition of men.' The whole commandment of God is the commandment to love.

90

Laws, whether imposed by the Church or by the State, restrict man's freedom only under one condition: where love is lacking. Without the love of God to simplify and give meaning to the principle whereby man rules over man, life is hedged about with burdensome controls. Instead of freeing him, these laws enslave him. The natural man feels frustrated. His every movement is made at the will of another, and he resents not being his own master. Not so the man who loves, who sees in the petty as well as in the significant demands of obedience the loving will of God. For him the more ways in which God expresses his authority the better. Instead of enslaving him to rules, God's rule frees him from the tyranny of self. Every external act of submission springs from an internal act of offering, of fealty, and the emphasis is now not upon the terms of this or that obedience but upon the spirit of obedience which is properly the spirit of love.

So it is love, and only love, which makes man free. It is love which St James is writing about when he uses, with strict accuracy, the term 'law of liberty'. To some the phrase 'law of liberty' suggests a contradiction. How could law be other than restrictive? But St James knew what he was talking about.

There is nothing so liberating as the law of Christ's love.

Apply all this to actual practice. In following the Mass as recommended, in falling in with the Sunday sermon, in denying yourself the pleasure of the banned entertainment, you are not so much adding still more burdens to your Catholicism as finding still more outlets to your love. You can afford to forget about the legal side of it, and can concentrate instead upon the side which invites you to service. There is all the difference in the world between service and servitude.

91

We can easily tell if we have missed the point about the relationship between law and love. Are rules an end in themselves for us, and is our obedience given to the machinery of power rather than to the source of power? If we get the principle of obedience wrong, mistaking subservience to a system for service to a Person, we are liable to get other principles wrong in the spiritual life. Obedience is bound up with charity, humility, and penance. Once again it is a question of arriving at the attitude of mind by means of prayer. Prayer correlates the virtues and teaches the soul how to keep the right balance.

Before he has taken on the life of prayer, a man would not believe it possible that he could ever come to *like* surrendering his own will in obedience. He is prepared to do his best, but he looks upon it as a necessary evil, as the debt he owes to truth. But when he begins to live spiritually he finds that laws bring peace. He does not have to drive himself to do what the rules say or what a superior commands: he is only too glad to be given such a clear-cut manifestation of God's will. Everything else in his life may be uncertain and dark, but here anyway he knows where he is. It makes him feel free, at home, grateful.

This is only what you would expect if God is love, and if he is expressing himself through the medium of delegated authority. Yet most of us do not expect it. Even with the light of prayer to help us, we can be caught off our guard, and when this happens it is always because we have seen the intermediary not as representing a greater authority but as coming at the end of the line. Somewhat in the way that charity brings about its own order in the soul (*ordinavit in me caritatem*), prayer steers the soul from natural to supernatural obedience. It orders the soul's response in a measured ascent of love.

92

Prayer does not come to the rescue by shining upon our human problems as though trained from a searchlight. Seldom is a difficulty caught in a beam, shown up against the surrounding darkness, and given the appropriate solution. More usually the process is so indirect and so gradual that we tend not to connect the outcome with the fact that we have been praying for it. We forget that grace, working through nature, is not likely to appear *as* grace.

Perhaps this is one reason why we are slow to show gratitude when our prayers are answered: we see a sequence of natural events with their material causes, and conclude that what we wanted has taken place—would have taken place anyway—without any help from God. God in fact makes a twofold bid for our faith, eliciting in the first instance the act which puts the matter in his hands, and in the second the recognition of his part in the satisfactory outcome.

By failing to give the supernatural interpretation to what appears to be a purely natural configuration of events, we miss an opportunity of faith, love, and worship. The challenge is not to meet this or that outward circumstance with stoicism, but to see in it the providential will of God. Do I watch God's finger tracing the course of my life, or do I put everything short of a manifestly divine intervention down to good management, fluke, coincidence, normal development? Prayer takes the natural contingencies into consideration, but gives them their supernatural orientation. To gather up the happenings of life, whether they are planned or haphazard, and to put them in their supernatural setting, is something we are given the grace to do. It requires neither heroism nor intellectual ability. It is only to recognize what in fact is true.

93

To recognize truth, and still more to apply it in the affairs of life, assumes a certain integrity of soul to begin with. While the human mind cannot stop searching for truth, it can very well reject it if the implications are found to be inconvenient.

The human mind is a restless, questing, unsatisfied instrument, and is the whole time looking for a formula which will cover all. It awaits a definition, an illumination, a compulsion of sorts which will clear up everything and establish certainty for ever. Eventually it is borne in upon the human mind that in this life such security cannot be, and that the best course is to make do as best it can with faith.

Then prayer steps in and helps. Used now, together with the will, as a vehicle of prayer, the mind no longer bothers about finding a formula which will be comprehensive. It knows that the nearest thing to a completely satisfying definition is love, but that even love, as it is experienced in our limited human condition, does not provide the whole answer. The mind's exercise henceforward is accordingly to stretch out to God in prayer, and to others in understanding and compassion.

It is a curious fact that just when the mind has despaired of finding satisfaction anywhere, it finds its only satisfaction in the one exercise, namely prayer, which of its nature promises no satisfaction in this life anyway. If there were no other argument for the existence of grace, this might well prove it. When it addresses itself to prayer, the human mind labours under disadvantages so vast as to *need* the influence of grace if it is to get anywhere at all. Without grace, St Paul tells us, we cannot even call upon the name of Jesus.

94

Admission of its limitations, almost one might say of its disqualifications, is the mind's best claim to divine assistance. 'When I am weak,' said St Paul, 'then am I strong . . . virtue is made perfect in infirmity.' So when we know we can do nothing, we are well placed for doing something; when we are convinced of our foolishness, we are wiser than the wise. Not until our supports are kicked from under us and we are left suspended in the air, is there anything solid—the paradox is as sharp as that—on which to build.

By a long and painful process we come to know our nothingness, and it is then that we have to rely upon God to supply our lack. There is nothing else we can do: we cannot generate our own strength. 'No other foundation does man have but that which is laid, which is Christ Jesus.' As the foundation is Christ, so what is built on it must be Christ. We have to learn our nothingness at first hand, and then we have to learn, also at first hand, the power of Christ.

It is not difficult to see why St Benedict makes so much of humility. He has been called *doctor humilitatis*. Of all the virtues, humility is the most elusive. When you think you have got it, you find it has turned into its opposite. Certainly you learn far more about it by praying and loving than by performing humiliations and telling people how worthless you are. St Paul's texts might be put in reverse: 'when I feel myself to be strong, then am I weak . . . weakness declares itself in the assumption of strength.'

95

It is worth noting how often St Paul warns against complacency. 'He who thinks himself to stand, let him take heed lest he fall.' It is a law of the spiritual life that our greatest humiliations and failures come hard upon the heels of our supposed triumphs. In this connection, and by way of keeping ourselves in our place, we do well to well to consider a fairly common occurrence among devout people: the sudden *volte face* which abandons the life of prayer and plunges into worldliness.

By what mental process does someone whose whole interest for months, perhaps for years, has been religion, lapse overnight? How can people who have comfortably spent hours before the Blessed Sacrament, who delight in retreats, who read spiritual books, who fast and get up early for Mass, suddenly drop off and get married outside the Church or take to drink? Has the life of grace had no effect, then, that when the test comes there is a cool choice away from it?

One's immediate reaction to such a situation is to assume that the zest for prayer was all put on, and that the prayer itself was sheer delusion. But this need not be the true explanation. *Any* turning towards God in prayer must derive its impulse from grace, so at least in the beginning the move was genuine. What it means is that somewhere along the line there was the temptation to indulge either sloth or vain glory. Both these weaknesses can be corrected, but until they are corrected they play havoc with the spiritual life. There is really no problem as regards sloth because the remedy is patently obvious, but in the case of vain glory—striking the man-of-prayer attitude—there is greater danger. As a rule it is this which accounts for the apparently sudden moral and spiritual collapse.

96

It is not unreasonable to presume that the powers of evil, aware of what promises to be a generous service of God, go out of their way to divert the zealous beginner. The more seasoned soul will have a different catalogue of temptations to handle, but for the neophyte the likeliest temptation is that of vain glory. Deprived of the glory which was expected before the soul got under way, the novice in his disappointment opts for a false glory, glory at any price.

By sitting about in church all day, and refusing to pay the price of this luxury with a self-denial which would act as the necessary astringent, the soul feeds on vanity. The image of my-ever-recollected-self becomes so inflated as to leave little room for true prayer. Humility is lost sight of, and hypocrisy rules the day.

Fortunately there is always the chance of turning hypocrisy back into humility. Since there is nothing so humiliating as the knowledge that one is a hypocrite, the way back, if one would only take it, is made easy. Moreover the way back should be made additionally easy when it is understood that those prayers which were offered to God at the beginning, and even those prayers which were offered when the soul was posing as a spiritual person, are not just so much scrap. They had a value of a sort because they had a direction of a sort, and in humbly going back to begin the spiritual life on firmer foundations, the soul can pick them up and offer them again to God. No prayer, however mismanaged, is utterly wasted and useless. (Prayer to commit sin is no prayer.)

97

We are not told that the pharisee's prayer was matter for guilt, but that the publican's was better. The pharisee was vain, pompous, lacking in charity—all this weighing against him in disposing for prayer—but because he was a hypocrite, it does not follow that his prayer was accounted a lie. He had set out to talk to God, and talk to God he did. It was just that he talked about the wrong things. His prayer, for what it was worth, fell within the definition of prayer. The publican 'went down into his house justified *rather than* the other'. St Luke chooses his words carefully.

Who in his prayer does not share with the pharisee an element of humbug? Who does not find in his prayer more of the pharisee's hypocrisy than of the publican's humility? But so long as there remains a shred of good intention, there is the accompanying grace to move up from insincerity to sincerity. Even though the sham may have gained over the true, this is not necessarily so of every moment during the prayer. A prayer is still a real prayer even when it has been made by a sham person.

So provided the repudiation of the original intention has not been substantial, and vain glory has not absolutely taken over, there is still a margin in which grace can operate. Indeed God can use a soul's infidelity, even apostasy, to bring about an altogether new attitude of heart. Otherwise there would be no room in the Church for the penitent. In the case of the man who has lapsed, the initial attraction to the things of the spirit was not, whatever the scandalised may say, a delusion. The life of prayer was not, while it lasted, merely window-dressing. The undertaking may have been tainted with self—whose is not?—but there was enough grace in it to make possible a reorientation according to the earlier intention.

98

In the providence of God a failure to live up to the adventure of grace may be exactly what the soul needs. The lapse, this apparently fatal experiment which causes scandal to others and desperation to oneself, can turn out to be a powerful factor in the soul's sanctification. The test lies in what decision is made when the dust of apostasy settles. Continuation in infidelity or willingness to consider a return to grace.

So if the onetime man of prayer *does* throw over religion and go roaring off in the opposite direction, at least he need not be accused of being deceitful from the start. It means he has been sidetracked, possibly, but not necessarily, for good.

'This may to a certain extent excuse him,' might be the comment here, 'but how explain the suddenness which is often the most shocking feature of the defection? Holy Communion up till the last day, and not near a church since.' The answer is that of course the rejection has come at the end of many other rejections, and is not simply an isolated act.

99

People do not drop prayer and the sacraments as casually as they would drop a correspondence or cancel a library subscription. The whole idea of grace as a force which builds up the character and gives increasing light to those who look for it contradicts such a proposition. It goes clean against our idea of God to think that the faithful are more or less at the mercy of one quick overwhelming temptation, which, if they give in to it, may well wreck their chances of salvation. Surely the only other alternative is the correct one, namely that the soul, while outwardly appearing faithful, has made so many secret choices away from God that when a really significant choice come up for decision the appearances are thrown to the winds, and the fateful act of the will follows the direction of the rest.

The bridge collapses suddenly—but only because the piers have been gradually crumbling away. The supposedly healthy man drops dead in the street—but only because his disease has at last caught up on him. An electric wire bursts unexpectedly into flame—but only because its strands have become more and more frayed. Of the three analogies, that of the wire is the closest because its purpose is to conduct the very element which, when something goes wrong, makes for its destruction. Because grace has no other function but to promote the service of God, it is, when misused, a liability instead of an asset.

Examples can be found to illustrate this. Jeremias was established by the Lord to 'build up and lay low, to plant and uproot'. Christ's coming was 'for the salvation or reprobation of many in Israel'. And then the Blessed Sacrament: 'He who eats or drinks unworthily, eats and drinks damnation to himself'. God's blessings have a way of turning themselves inside out when they are not received according to the intention of the donor.

100

It was not because of a hasty muddleheadedness, pardonable in the excitement of a wedding night, that the foolish virgins found themselves locked out. It was because, knowing what was required of them and warned in good time, they expected to get by on their appearance as bridesmaids. If we imagine that our status as souls of prayer entitles us to entry into the kingdom of heaven we are mistaken. It is not the status that counts, but the love which verifies the status.

Though all are called to love, and therefore to the life of prayer, not all are expected to make prayer their life's work. The service of God includes, but is not restricted to, prayer. There must be countless people living in the world who become holy on less than half the amount of prayer which is demanded of most religious. By doing the work which he is equipped by God to do, a man gives glory to God and becomes holy. 'Live according to what you are,' is the scholastic axiom, 'and you will grow.' While everyone is equipped for the service of God which leads to high sanctity, not everyone is endowed with the particular kind of graces which lead to transforming union with God in prayer.

Live according to what you are. What am I? I am a servant of God, and if I ever fulfil myself it will be as a soul of prayer and charity. It is not enough merely to like the idea of praying always and loving everyone. I must be ready to put aside everything that gets in the way of actually doing these things. The obstacles, so far as they can be foreseen, must be avoided absolutely. We are talking now of a particular ideal. There are other ideals which a man is free to follow—patriotism, education, integration, democracy and what not—but here it is a question of one. The ideal of love summons to a way of thinking, to a way of trusting, to a way of living. The summons is not to specific exercises, but to that colour of mind which informs and directs every exercise.

101

It is not always easy to know what label to tie to our particular brand of service. Many well-intentioned people form a clear picture of the ideal which they want to follow for the love of God, but fail to relate the objective to the subjective: they leave their own temperament out of account. They take endless trouble (and give endless trouble) to secure a way of life which looks ideal on paper (and *is* ideal for some people) but to which their natures are unsuited. God has given us one kind of nature, and we have to find out how he means us to use it. To force it into a mould which we would make for ourselves if we were God is to go against not only our God-given nature, but, more importantly, to go against God's will.

For example many souls feel the lure of the eremitical life. They know that to be a hermit is one of the highest vocations given to man. But to live alone with God is a very rare vocation, and few are psychologically and spiritually qualified to follow this way. Most of those who try and fail at being hermits are victims of the delusion that if you want a thing badly enough God will accommodate himself to your wishes. Vanity comes into it too. Even some of those who grimly hang on to their own will and manage to persevere as hermits, sacrificing a much more fruitful service which they could give by not being hermits, do so because of something which is not of the essence of the hermit vocation.

Vocation is a very subtle matter, and nobody seems to have explained it satisfactorily. The only conclusion to be drawn is that sincerity and openmindedness are the qualities most necessary if the call from God is to be understood in his terms. Instead of asking 'What do I want to do with my life?' it is better first to ask 'What does God want me to do with my life?' If he has different ideas from me, it will lead only to unhappiness and unholiness if I press my own. It is safer to be in a life which I do not choose, but which is God's will, than to be in a life which I do choose, but which is not God's will. When people said what a wonderful vocation it must be to be the mother of Christ, our Lord told them that in fact the most wonderful vocation was to know the will of God and do it.

102

Nothing is so misleading in the search for one's true vocation as the romantic associations which can be attached to almost any form of the service of God. Scornful of the prosaic realities, the soul selects the glamourous accidentals with which to stiffen the resolve to see the thing through, and then, when the life is actually lived, there is disillusion. When a man fashions a vocation for himself it is no longer a vocation.

Since the whole point of a vocation is that it comes from God, and, if it is responded to, will be lived by the power of

God, the pictures which a man paints of it in his mind cannot be expected to coincide with the essential concept as it exists in the mind of God. The two are on different levels, and until the human mind is ready to rid itself of the imaginary it cannot properly get hold of the real.

A thirteenth century Cistercian writer mentions the *spiritus fictionis* which bedevils the monastic vocation, conjuring up a life led in picturesque cloisters and among whispering trees. Cardinal Newman, with his reference to the 'poetry' of the monk's quiet calling, has done nothing to dispel this idea. But it is not only the solitary and the cenobite whose respective service is misunderstood by false advertisement: the missionary, the nurse, the worker among the poor, the political reformer, the mother of a family, the teacher. Every walk of life can be unrealistically presented.

103

In order to see themselves in the role God means them to play, souls have need of humility. Reminding us not only of our origins but also of our lowly condition, whatever the gifts God has given us, the word is derived from *humus,* earth. We do not have to fly high to find God's will: it is lying all about us on the ground. We can take warning from the thought that Icarus fell from the skies because his wings were stuck on with wax.

Peace in one's vocation is not to be won by deceit. While few deliberately deceive themselves about what they are looking for, many would find their true vocation more quickly if they guarded against the self-deception which is in good faith. The mind can be in two places at once, the real and the unreal, so the more it renounces the unreal the greater its claim to the will of God. Nothing is more real than the will of God.

When someone projects himself into a part which is not his own he thereby contracts out of the part for which God has cast him. This is why spiritual writers come out strongly against the habit of day-dreaming. As a mere act of the imagination there is nothing wrong with day-dreaming—any more than as a mere act of the memory there is anything wrong in going over the past. But when the imagination transports from reality to unreality, making the fiction more real than the fact, there can be trouble. In the same way when the memory leads to dwelling more in the past than in the present there can be trouble.

104

Our safety lies in taking ourselves as we are, faults and all, and handing over the material to God. The faults he can correct far more effectively than we can, and whatever good qualities we possess are his to develop as he pleases. Some possess so-called strong characters, others so-called weak. It is not the distinction between strong and weak that matters; what matters is the shaping of character according to God's will. According to grace.

Some people are calm by nature, patient, reliable, confident, interested in people and in the world about them. Good luck to them. They have much to offer to God, much to be thankful for, much on which grace can work. Others are naturally restless, unsure of themselves and of everything else, unpredictable, intraverted, melancholy. These have just as much to offer to God, and it will probably cost them more to do it. It is idle to compare one kind of person with another, and estimate respective values. It is equally idle to put ourselves in one or other category. The only thing which qualifies is the response which is given to grace, and since we have no way of measuring this, either in our own case or anyone else's, it is wiser to leave it and get on with serving God.

Accepting ourselves for what we are must not be interpreted as an excuse to indulge our weaknesses. On the contrary it means resisting them. There are two kinds of admission: the wrong kind which says 'I am made like this and there is nothing I can do about it', and the right kind which says 'I know the kind of person I am, and it is very humbling, but I refuse to be discouraged, because God knows me better than I do and can give me the grace I need to meet my particular limitations.'

105

Prayer does not alter a person's nature, but it makes all the difference to his disposition. I cannot hope that I shall be miraculously changed from a congenitally sad person to a jolly one, but I can confidently hope that by being faithful to the light I receive in prayer I shall be at peace with the temperament that has been given me, and shall not be a man with a grievance. What has been a bad disposition for the interior life is turned into a good one.

So the soul of prayer does not worry over much about his nature. He takes it for granted. What causes him more concern is his disposition as regards grace. If he can keep himself flexible to the movement of the Holy Spirit, denying God nothing deliberately, he knows that God will do the rest. He does not ask to see progress: this is not his business. His business is to dispose himself.

People complicate the interior life unduly by wanting to classify their reactions to grace, to take soundings of their souls, to compute their spiritual output. They feel there must be a required standard, and are always trying to find out how near they have got to it.

106

We tend to imagine that the call to the interior life follows a set pattern. Whether the vocation is to take vows in religion or to remain in the world, we are fairly sure at the outset that it is a question of steering a straight course and keeping up the pace. The result will be spiritual progress. In other words we see it as what we do for God instead of as what God does in us. 'I have only to follow the instructions step by step and I'll end up where I want to be.' It is not quite as straightforward as this.

The books give recognised stages, and sometimes a learner will be granted to see what stage he is in, but for the most part it is a zigzag process which has all the appearances of a muddle. This it is which makes the whole thing such a venture of faith. It is a business of groping inch by inch all the way: nothing seems to conform to standard. It is more chaotic than most secular adventures, and consists mostly in waiting for something to happen which does not happen. There is nothing in the world so exhausting as waiting.

Waiting and loneliness nearly always go together. If this is so in the natural order it is so also in the supernatural order. Go over your past and pick out the occasions when you have waited for a telephone call, when you have watched the clock for a visit which did not come, for a train to arrive. In mature life we have become schooled to disappointment, but in the spiritual life we never seem to mature and are consequently forever at the mercy of loneliness and disappointment. We await God, but he does not come. With the psalmist we cry: 'Hear me quickly, Lord, for my spirit flags.' Failing the object of our desire, we are bewildered, despairing, lost. 'What is there upon earth that I look for apart from you?' we echo the psalmist's words, 'you alone are my inheritance.'

107

The feeling that one may have to wait for God's presence for the rest of one's life and that there is no guarantee that one will find it when one is dead, the conviction that no progress is being made and that God is not faintly interested in whether it is or not, the sense of waste accompanied by the firm belief that somewhere there must be something worth while and true: these things combine effectively to test one's faith.

It is all in the psalter. 'Why have you forgotten me at long last? . . . when will you return? . . . you have made me to dwell in darkness as those who are long dead . . . my spirit within me is afraid, my heart desolate and alone . . . I stretch out my hands to you, and as the parched earth my soul thirsts for your presence . . . let me soon taste of your mercy for my spirit is wasting away.' From the New Testament we get the same cry of anxious longing in Mary of Bethany's 'They have taken away my Lord and I know not where they have put him.'

In the life of prayer such opposites as doubt and faith, turmoil and peace, dread and hope, sorrow and joy are reconciled. The soul develops the habit of stepping over the emotions and refusing to allow anything to invade the area where God's will is the sole consideration. This does not mean living in a dream world, indifferent to human affairs, and giving to God a bloodless service in which the suppression of passion is the highest virtue. It means living in the will despite the passions. It means carrying the passions before God and laying them at his feet in faith. There is nothing bloodless and dehumanised about this.

108

When it is possible to supernaturalize our doubts, turmoils, dreads and sorrows, it is a wasteful mistake to rationalize them. Psychoanalysis can find excuses for most of our griefs and unenviable appetites, and to a certain extent lessen their influence, but why ask science to make allowances for what God makes allowances for anyway? If we want our weaknesses condoned we have no right to ask for it, and if we expect them to be cured without the help of grace we shall be disappointed. While it is true that the confessional cannot always do duty for the consulting-room, and that the sciences of mind and body may legitimately be drawn upon, trust in God must be considered before all else.

It is not strange that good Christian people when made sorrowful with doubts and dreads will try every sort of remedy —tranquilizers, alcohol, change of scene, shock treatment— before they give the life of prayer a chance? Often they are deterred from applying this solution by the idea that prayer will aggravate their trouble, will heighten the tension and bring about a nervous condition. But far from adding to the strain, prayer brings peace.

Though the glory of God and not peace of mind is the first object of prayer, the fact that the soul is making an act of trust has a calming effect. To have handed over one's problems to God for solution, knowing that there is no sorrow which Christ has not experienced, brings not only relief but a sense of kinship with the Son of God. 'Peace be to you' said Christ to his disciples as he showed them his hands and his feet.

109

Peace. It means different things to different people. To certain rare souls it may mean being ready to do without it, but to most ordinary souls of prayer it is something which comes when they have looked squarely at life's defeats and accepted them without resentment. It is not a matter of becoming more philosophical or less hopeful; it is a matter of not straining after peace any more, and seeing it rather in a state of soul than of mind. It has more to do with confidence than with tranquillity. While outward tranquillity and inward peace should normally go together there is no necessary connection.

So inward peace and agitation are not mutually exclusive terms. 'My peace I give unto you, not as the world gives.' The peace of Christ—his gift which is built up by faith and prayer —is not to be measured against nerves, overwork, lack of leisure. It resides deep in the soul. A lot of nonsense is talked about peace. People seem to imagine that the soul of prayer is peaceful in the sense of being impervious to emotional upset. But souls of prayer, and therefore of peace, are subject to emotional stresses like everyone else. But they do not get excited about them: they do not allow worries, temptations, fears and so on to swamp their confidence in God.

This peacefulness of spirit, then, means being at one with life as God gives it. It means faith and love. In the last analysis the man who is in a state of grace is in the state of peace: God, the author of true peace, is dwelling within him. But it does not do to analyse one's enjoyment of peace, because, like happiness, it is shy of the microscope. Try to pin down your peace, accounting for it and testing its reactions, and you being to wonder whether you possess as much of it as you thought. The best way to maintain peace is to forget about it, concentrating instead upon the prayer and trust which cause it.

110

There are those who claim that they can detect the authentic quality of peace in other people, particularly of course in people with a reputation for holiness, but one wonders if the claim is valid. The presence of peace can be simulated, and the absence of peace can be misleading. This is not to discount the value of serenity, which can be a sign of sanctity, but merely to question its visibility.

Since it rests upon the life of grace, which in any case defies scientific investigation, the question of evaluating peace is best left to God. *In la sua voluntade e nostra pace* says Dante in the *Purgatorio,* which can be taken to mean that most of us look for it in the wrong place so do not know it when we see it.

'If this peace you speak about is as elusive as all that' it might be objected, 'and can remain unfelt, does it very much matter if one has got it or not?' The answer is like that given by a broadcasting corporation to the listeners' complaints about the commercials being so much louder than the scheduled programmes: 'The volume is the same; it is just that they *sound* louder.' Peace only *feels* unfelt. One is aware of it all right when it is threatened by sin.

111

Closely connected with peace, so closely that it is sometimes mistaken for it, is patience. Again a possibly authentic mark of sanctity, again a quality born of prayer and the spiritual life. The mistake is to think of patience in the negative sense as the suppression of irritability. Self-control is a good start but more positively patience is longsuffering: continuance in accepting the will of God. Patience as treated here is accordingly considered in relation to God's order rather than to exasperation. This is the kind of patience you find in St Paul. 'In whatever state I am, I am content therewith.'

A truly patient person, one who has acquired the habit of it through fidelity to grace, can be angry without losing patience. This sounds absurd, but understood as contentment with one's condition whatever the mood, patience need not be affected by a burst of anger. Some of the saints—St Jerome, for instance, and St Thomas of Canterbury—were by nature hot tempered. No blame to them. If the saints were not men of spirit they would never fight hard enough in their pursuit of holiness. 'The kingdom of heaven suffers violence, and only the violent bear it away.'

If peace can coexist with struggle and upset, patience can coexist with violent action prompted by indignation. Our Lord, who never lost patience for an instant and demanded that we follow him in his meekness which he preached as a beatitude, was very angry in the temple and resorted to violence. Christ did not lack spirit: as man he was one of stronge emotions. Patience and even passion—in Christ's case 'pro-passion'—can go together.

112

Trials, whether temporal or spiritual, are taken by the patient man for what they are: namely tests planned by God's providence and not miseries of chance imposed by vengeful human conditions. The naturally patient man has much to be thankful for, and the supernaturally patient man has even more. True patience is a work of grace. *Quoniam tu es Domine spes mea* says the psalmist with strict accuracy.

Supernatural patience, a disposition built up by grace, rides the storm. It may ride it awkwardly, showing flashes of irritation, but shakes off the disgruntled habit of mind. It perseveres in endurance and specialises in humility. It is tolerant with regard to ourselves, with regard to others, with regard to circumstances, and above all with the way by which God is leading us.

Patience means forbearance with the folly, malice, injustice, and waste which is in the world. It sees these things in terms of eternity, so can afford to take its time. Patience never judges, is never dismissive, is never cynical, goes on having confidence in human nature, is always accessible, always ready to be put upon. Patience puts up with the bore, the humbug, the so-called undeserving, the trickster. Seen in such terms, patience is a necessary part of charity.

113

After our Lord himself, the pattern of patience may be seen in our Lady. She, the queen of patience, would have had to endure not only the endless frustration of living in a world which refused to recognise her son, but, after his death, the hideous delay before she was allowed to join him in heaven.

Yes, but Mary was immaculately conceived. It was different for her. What about us? We feel a mounting rage when we hear about the corruption of the young, about concentration camps in Christian countries, about segregation in Catholic parishes. How do you expect us to be patient as our Lady was patient?

Again, as in the case of peace, it is a question of a settled, deep down, deliberately directed attitude towards life. It may or may not appear to others, and, cost what it may to acquire and practise, it will hardly appear as anything very meritorious to us. Indeed it would spoil the whole thing if we were able to congratulate ourselves upon being models of patience. It is another of these hidden virtues, so hidden that we are not aware of it. One is reminded of the incident in *Alice* where the White King is waiting for his courtiers. 'I see nobody on the road' says Alice. 'What wonderful eyesight' says the King, 'to be able to see nobody—and from such a long way off.' The virtuous man is often pushed by God into a position from which he can see nothing, nobody, and not the least virtue in himself.

114

Not only are virtues unseen by the person possessing them but their very opposites are seen and deplored with deep compunction. 'We see diminishment, both in us and around us,' writes Pere Teilhard de Chardin, 'which does not seem to be compensated by advantages at any perceptible level . . . how can these diminishments which are altogether without compensation, wherein we see death at its most deathly, become for us a good?'

It becomes for us a good precisely because it *seems* to us such a devastating bad. The development is occasioned by the destruction. The healing force comes into play by occasioning death. The seed has to die if it is to live, the man must lose his life if he is to find it, the rose-bush has to be cut if it is to produce its best roses, food is submitted to burning or boiling if it is not to be served raw, rockets have to endure an explosion at the launching pad if they are to mount into space.

So it is often the case in the spiritual life that what looks like, and feels like, the betrayal of a virtue is in fact, because of the temptations against it which kick up a disturbance, an exercise of the virtue at a new level. The old expressions are reversed. Where up till now the virtue was maintained by removing as far as possible the obstacles to its exercise, now it is a matter of the virtue emerging *from* the obstacles. What sort of life it is that rises out of the ashes is not the soul's concern. It is for the soul to trust and not ask questions. It would ruin the work if we could admire our Phoenix, and keep it as a household pet.

115

Reaching the stage of not knowing where to turn, not daring to trust in the possession of character or virtue, the soul is faced with the straightforward choice between prayer and sin. Assuming that the right choice is made, there is no reason to believe that immediately the tension ceases and that peace results. What will happen is that faith will be strengthened.

Doubts will continue to harry the intellect, and evil desires will go on trying to loosen the foundations in the will, but so long as the soul remains faithful to prayer, God for his part cannot desert his own.

God has pledged himself not to allow us to be tempted beyond our capacity to resist, and provided we do not walk into the occasions of sin we are sure of the grace to reject temptation. What we have to recognize is that temptation will never be far away, and that the theological virtues, because they are the most vital of all the virtues, will come under particular attack.

Faith, hope, and charity are so closely interconnected that temptations against one are temptations against the other two. What is perhaps less generally recognised is that temptations which appear to be directed against purity, against moderation in eating and drinking, against justice and fortitude and patience, are often, in a subtle way, a more serious threat to faith, hope, and love. The immediate object of temptation may be the tendency to alcohol, sex, cruelty, sloth, but what the powers of evil are trying to achieve is the sense of despair which lets everything go.

116

The theological virtues are kept in condition by the sacraments and the exercise of prayer. It is by living the spiritual life that the soul comes to see what the grosser temptations are really getting at, and can take steps to guard against the first movements of evil. Where in the beginning the instinctive reaction to temptation was to stand up and fight, the reaction now is to lean more heavily on grace and therefore to take refuge in prayer and trust.

Self-indulgence for instance. Good resolutions are certainly worth making, but they are not likely to get to the root of the evil. If the person's character is weak enough to allow habits of self-indulgence, it is not likely to be strong enough to keep the good resolutions. So the indirect approach of prayer is far more likely to be effective. In prayer the character is built up, confidence in God is built up, humility and hope are built up. With such a disposition to work on, God supplies strength where there was weakness.

How, without prayer, can the limited human intelligence find its way in the complex world of right and wrong? Lacking prayer, the mind, heart, senses are fair game for the vastly superior intellect of the devil. Perhaps we do not enough appreciate the reality of a *personal* power of evil: a planning evil mind whose whole business it is to falsify truth and trap us, individually, into committing sin.

117

It is not only sin that spoils everything. Temptation, by showing us how eggshell frail are our natural defenses, can spoil everything too. The uncertainty of our reserves, the transience of our enjoyment, the apparent futility of our effort, the variable nature of our service, the bleakness of our future, the doubts about our religious allegiance: all these things make happiness, material or spiritual, a pretty chancy thing. The mistake is to conclude from it that life is no more than a series of haphazard, idle, meaningless events, that it is a time sequence at once fortuitous and inescapable, that it is tied to a pattern arbitrarily devised and relentlessly impersonal. This in effect is the great temptation, because it points to cynicism and despair.

Without prayer to give another side to the phenomenon of failure, such an understanding of life would not be such a very unnatural one to follow. But prayer, by looking into the distances of faith, gives an altogether new perspective. The fortuitous is seen to have purpose after all, the wasted can be viewed as providing opportunity later on, the trivial is understood to be vastly important. Life, if prayer and faith get it right for us, is not the mess we have made it but the opportunity which God has made it.

Only when the soul comes to live in Christ does life reveal its opportunity. Touching the will of God, the soul touches reality, and when the will of God is fulfilled from moment to moment the true significance of God's outward order is recognized. Truth is nowhere apart from the will of God. It is because the world is satisfied with half truths that it remains only half interested in the will of God. Except to the surface appearances, the world stays uncommitted.

118

While not wholly materialistic, the world does not take its stand on supernatural verities. It sets great store by justice, fellowship, fortitude, obedience to law, education, hospitality, but is shy of bearing witness to religion's strictly spiritual realities. There is every likelihood here that the natural virtues not only take precedence of the supernatural virtues but actually get in their way. Thus the policies of the welfare state can be opposed to the principles of religion and the supernatural life. So it is the duty of the man of prayer to stand back from his social environment and examine the tenets of contemporary civilization. For example he must question the means advocated in dealing with the population explosion, with unhappy marriages, with strikes, with prisoners of war, and with war itself.

In his own personal life the man of prayer will need to assure himself that the supernatural, and not the natural, is his first objective. He may have a preference for truth above lying, for beauty above ugliness, for the genuine above the sham. But there is nothing particularly religious about this. Atheists feel the same. You do not have to be religious to like goodness and dislike badness. Fastidiousness is no substitute for supernatural religion.

What the man of prayer has to ask himself is whether he really loves good and hates evil—as God understands them. Does he hunger after the will of God, and not merely after good order, world peace, happiness for all? It is in the interests of falsehood that we mistake the superficially desireable for what God means us to desire. In good faith we can hanker after better conditions when with stronger faith we should be hankering after God's conditions. We should not stop short at benevolence when God is calling us to love. Natural inclination may incline us to benevolence, but it is grace that moves us to supernatural charity.

119

The main source of confusion in the spiritual life springs less from our sins—which we can see and be sorry for—than from our mistaken approaches. For example we can go for years practising prayer for no better reason than that we mean to be souls of prayer. Where has the glory of God come in? We can go on for years doing kind acts for no better reason than that we should qualify as souls of charity. Where has the love of Christ come in? The same may be said of our penance and our humility: we have practised the works of these virtues because of the label attaching to them.

In this way the gifts which God has given us for a particular purpose, namely to strengthen union with himself, are frittered away in the service of self. The desire to be classified as this or that kind of soul in the service of God does more harm than a straightforward worldly ambition. While to dream of high office is readily seen to be inconsistent with the interior life, and can be laughed out of the system, the dream of high sanctity for the edification of all is felt to be almost part of the commitment and is certainly no joke.

It requires the light of grace to distinguish between what has been embarked upon because of the cachet which comes with it and what is, irrespective of cachet, chosen for the love of God. The light may reveal such deviations as to demand of the soul a fresh start on altogether new lines. A test here: either I content myself with the mediocrity which has been my state for as long as I can remember—and now that I have seen where my mistake lay, I shall be following a more imperfect course than before—or else face the implication of this new-found self-knowledge, and aim anew at perfection. And this time it must be God's idea of perfection.

120

The spiritual life means facing a crossroads of one kind or another at almost every step of the way. The search after perfection is something which has to be renewed each morning, and in the act of searching there has always to be a deciding, a choosing. We have to make up our minds not to go back, not to take the easy way out, not to rest in the superficial. And on the positive side we have to choose God's will even when we have not the remotest notion what it is or where it will lead us. 'Thy will be done'—and then blind trust.

In another sense too the spiritual life is a crossroads: we are either allowing our victories over self, such as they are, to go to waste or we are acknowledging our defeats, and are thereby turning them into victory. In other words we either walk gayly and unconcerned along the road of self-deception or else we face reality which means shame. In theory it looks simple enough, and when presented with the alternative we know that, whatever the humiliation, we must opt for truth. But in practice it is a vastly different matter.

The trouble is that even when the right choice has been made, there is no assurance that anything has been achieved. This is just where faith comes in, because were we to congratulate ourselves upon having answered the summons of grace we would appropriate to ourselves the merit of having done the generous thing. Nothing so satisfies the ego as to have been proved generous, faithful, loving. Consequently we must be ready, as St Teresa of Lisieux says, to offer to God not only the fruit of the tree but the tree itself.

121

It is only in offering to God—offering tree as well as fruit —that the soul finds any sort of real peace. Peace, someone has said, comes in proportion to the things which we can do without. Our Lord promises spiritual things in return for the renunciation of material ones. New lamps for old. But there is this to be noted: it is detachment and not disenchantment that is blessed by God. We are not to despise the good things of God's creation, and still less are we to offer him (as Cain did) the things which we have grown tired of or which are stale and bruised, but to use them sparingly. It is one thing to deny the good where we see it, and another to deny ourselves the use of it. We must confess to the good of God's creation, but be careful as to how we enjoy it.

Since standards of living change quickly, and differ from country to country, it would be rash to lay down a rule about what may be possessed. Nevertheless poverty is not, even in this age, not an outworn ideal. Renunciation of material satisfactions must still find a place in the spirituality of any period. It is today harder than ever for a singleminded searcher after God to steer a course between luxury on the one hand and ostentatious asceticism on the other. The creature comforts are there for the asking, and if he denies himself their use he will be charged with masochism.

It shames us sometimes to reflect upon the demands which

are made upon people in secular walks of life when we, with all our talk of renunciation for the love of God, live at ease. We who aspire after spirituality should compare our lot with that of the dedicated artist, communist, welfare worker. People will do even for money or for their figures what they would hardly do for God.

122

While comparisons are never wholly satisfactory, they can be useful in exposing the hollowness of certain assumptions. Thus to compare the earnest Christian with the earnest atheist may profitably shake us out of our complacency. Do we not take it for granted that singlemindedness is all on our side and that the atheist has blinded himself to the light? Is this quite fair? Often our opponents are more ready than we to suffer persecution for principle's sake.

In the purely interior field too, the sceptic may well outmatch us. Where we suffer agonies of doubt, the conscientious sceptic may for all we know suffer worse agonies of belief, and where we are tempted to despair of eternal life he may be tempted to hope in it. Not for us to adopt a superior attitude, looking down upon the benighted. Rather we should be humbled, admiring the staunchness of those who cannot command a particle of the help which is ours by grace of baptism.

If the above should seem farfetched it is only because the extreme has been singled out for example. Not so exaggerated is the comparison between spiritually-minded Catholics and the equally sincere followers of other creeds. How do we show up against the Buddhists, Hindus, Moslems, and more immediately against the votaries of other Christian churches? We do not possess the monopoly of charity and contemplation, and it is perhaps because we give ourselves such airs about these things that others outside our body are not drawn to join us in their exercise.

123

Not only in charity and contemplation are we often outclassed by members of other faiths but also in the matter of detachment. Whether they belong to a faith or not, a great number of people have to get along without material possessions anyway, and of these a great number are content with their condition. It puts us to shame when, with all our lofty notions about holy poverty, we come across unbelievers who are detached, unenvious, resigned.

We forget that detachment is an integral part not only of the interior life but of the ordinary down-to-earth Christian life. 'How hardly shall they who have riches find entry into the kingdom of heaven.' We have to place our treasure where rust and moth cannot reach . . . we must love not the world as the rich man Lazarus loved it . . . we are wrong to worry about temporal things, because our Father who is in heaven knows well that we have need of . . . our mistake is that of the rich young man whose great possessions caused him to turn down a vocation.

While not all are called to religious poverty, all are called to keep material things from getting the upper hand. Moreover all are called to share their possessions when others are in need, believing that man is the steward of God's gifts and not their master. Looked at from this point of view, riches are a blessing and not the curse that many have made them out to be. Riches can of course corrupt—leading to hardness of heart, ostentation, envy, pride, and any number of other unpleasant qualities —but there is no intrinsic reason why they should. Where the background is that of charity and prayer, wealth can be the most powerful instrument for good. Just because we may not worship money there is no reason why we should despise it. Nothing that God gives is to be spurned as an evil.

124

Detachment and mortification are not the same thing, but if it is being properly handled, mortification should lead to detachment. For this reason alone, though there are others, mortification is not something which can be discounted in the spiritual life. But in what is quaintly known as the civilized world, it is something which has come to be practised less and less. The subject can best be approached by way of the more generally understood requirement of the spiritual life, namely penance.

Man was redeemed from sin by Christ's act of atonement. By his passion and death Christ payed the debt which humanity owed to the Father. His was the perfect example of vicarious penance. But it did not stop at atonement: in its positive sense it was a summons, an invitation, a challenge. 'I, if I be lifted up, will draw all things to myself.' The crucifixion draws us to imitation as well as to Christ himself. His is in the strict sense an 'example': in our degree we are called to follow.

The call consequently is to love. 'Greater love than this no man has than that he lay down his life for his brethren.' So our penance, such as it is, is a surrendering of self in the name of love. How can we even pretend to rise to so high an ideal? Just because Christ has given the lead we have our answer to this question. As he takes over our prayers and makes them his, so he takes up our penances in the same way. Whatever penances we practise are valuable only to the degree that they find a place in Christ's passion, and are performed in his name.

125

The practical side of penance—that is the actual hardships and restrictions—is greatly simplified when we note the classical distinction between necessary and voluntary mortification. Under 'necessary' would come such remedial practices as would be needed to curb inordinate appetites and guard against concession to admitted weaknesses. Thus it is no act of supererogation to bridle gluttony, the sex instinct, love of money, a mania for gambling, the dedication to sport or entertainment or even work: these things have to be curbed anyway on pain of sinning by excess. But even necessary mortifications are meritorious, and though they amount to no more than avoiding the occasions of sin they can be performed to the glory of God.

While they look less heroic, necessary mortifications take precedence over the kind that are voluntary. For example before you take to hurling yourself into a bed of nettles you do better to put a ban on your uncharitable conversation. You need not think about sleeping on a board or fasting on bread and water until you have mortified your laziness, your love of gossip, your habit of smoking too much, your desire to attract attention.

Voluntary mortifications are those assumed at discretion

where the avoidance of sin does not arise. Such would be extra fasts, getting up in the night to pray, the use of hairshirts, chains, and disciplines. These would strictly be penances as distinct from mortifications, and to be of any merit in God's sight they would need the approval of authority. Finally there are the afflictions, trials, misunderstandings, temptations, losses and disappointments which come in the ordinary course of life. These can be very effective penances if we keep our wits about us and refer them to God as such. They have this great advantage over the voluntary kind that they do not provide fuel to our vanity. There can be a selfish satisfaction in having watched all night before the Blessed Sacrament, but there is not likely to be much satisfaction in the penance of being kept awake all night by the noise coming from the house next door.

126

It is a matter of concern to those especially who have the care of souls when suffering is seen to be wasted. Men and women who might be turning their afflictions over to God— who have only to unite themselves in spirit with Christ's passion —are found so often to stop short, and even to make of their trial further matter for selfishness. Even if we do not rebel positively against God's providential will, we can become so preoccupied with our troubles as to leave God out of account.

Instead of making us compassionate for others we can squander compassion on ourselves. Suffering is meant to enlarge our hearts, not shrink them. With suffering goes the grace of patience, peace, fortitude, penitence and love: all this can be missed if we make the mistake of turning in upon ourselves as the result of our trials.

To the Jews the cross was a stumbling-block and to the gentiles foolishness. What is it to us? Too often it can be an emblem merely, the significance of the symbol forgotten. The cross is something in which we are, by reason of our Christian inheritance, inextricably involved. Do we yield to it or harden ourselves against it? The cross is not just two planks fitted together on a certain day in the history of the world, and of all the relics which we venerate the most sacred, but a fact of our human experience which may or may not be sacred according to what we do about it.

127

It might be asked why so much attention is given to penance when prayer is manifestly more important. The answer is that without penance of some sort, prayer becomes either a pious luxury or a piece of humbug. Unless backed up with acts which correspond, the words of compunction which are addressed to God in prayer can hardly be sincere. Penance gives weight to prayer, becoming itself a prayer when performed with the right intention.

Only when penance is practised without prayer does it run off the lines. Penance can become an exaggeration, just as prayer can become an exaggeration, but in their joint response to grace, penance and prayer belong to the service of God in the way that mercy and love belong to the service of man. It is difficult to see how the one can be had without the other.

But always prayer comes first. It is prayer which brings light to bear upon penance, showing not only the value of mortification in general but in particular how to apply it under existing circumstances. It is in prayer that the soul normally feels drawn to this or that practice of penance, and it is prayer which secures its perseverance. St Paul makes an eloquent plea for penance where he points out that if an athlete has to deny himself when training for a race, we Christians should be able to do as much when the prize is eternal life in Christ.

128

The light to see one's way in the labyrinth of daily life, let alone in that of the spiritual life, comes as much through the liturgy as through private interior prayer. So much stress is laid upon the objective character of the liturgy that its personal function is often overlooked. Because of this artificial separation, the liturgy gets less support from interior souls than it deserves. Is it not a fact that the liturgy arouses among Catholics a variety of reactions ranging from peevish patronage to slavish addiction? Between these extremes you get more or less willing conformity, more or less tolerance, more or less openmindedness on points of controversy. Perhaps the liturgy would recommend itself more to the faithful of every shade if it were understood to have a personal private relevance as well as having a public task to perform.

In telling us that the Sabbath is made for man and not man for the Sabbath, our Lord is as good as saying that the liturgy is a means and not an end. This should settle the question, but apparently it does not. The trouble is that in spite of all the discussion about it, the liturgy is still a thing apart. It is not quite everyday prayer, and still less is it everyday life. And this is just the one thing which the present liturgical movement has tried to avoid. In time it may, but it has not yet.

When a means to an end is divided within itself it does not become two means but no means, and this is the danger today as regards the liturgy. The end of the liturgy is the greater glory of God: the means are the various liturgical forms. The means are composed of separate elements: biblical symbolism, historical fact and tradition, patristic and dogmatic theology, chant and ceremonial. To profit by this combined good presented by the liturgy, the human mind must be unprejudiced and ready to exercise itself. In the past, even if it has been unprejudiced, the Catholic mind has been slow to adapt itself. However ill-equipped we may be intellectually, we have no right to remain sluggish about the liturgy. It is everyone's concern, not merely that of the clergy and any who may feel its attraction.

129

One reason why many do not get what they should from the liturgy is that the nature of modern life has made them less receptive to ideas than they might be. Outward pressures, where they do not promote it, stifle thought. The liturgy proposes ideas which the majority excuse themselves from assimilating. 'We have managed up till now without falling into error and sin, so why do we have to learn all these new ways of thinking and praying?'

If we are to profit by what is offered us in the liturgy we must translate its propositions, though the medium of our personal prayer life, into terms which are both spiritual and applicable to contemporary conditions. The liturgy must *mean* something, not merely *proclaim* something. And mean something livable. We may or may not like the proclamation and the forms it takes, but we should try to get down to its real meaning.

The liturgy means love. How much it means love perhaps only our interior prayer, the prayer of faith, can teach us. But then the whole point of prayer is that we are ready to respond to the grace of the moment, and so to learn God's will. Whatever is done for God is done within the content of love.

130

In giving us a capacity for love, grace gives us a capacity for liturgical worship. Though it may not be given to all in the same degree, there is enough of the prepared condition in every baptised soul to make of the liturgy a reality. It is not a question of working up a feeling for the liturgy, or satisfying ligurgical requirements, or cramming in information about the liturgy; it is more a question of contactual assimilation. The soul has to be in sympathy, has to be *there*. If you think the liturgy expects you to toe the party line, you have got it wrong.

It is the liturgy's misfortune that it has been ·presented in an academic, appropriate-to-the-age, almost gimmicky sense. Indeed it is difficult to avoid these connotations. No external discipline can stimulate unless underlying it there is the impulse of a living tradition. Since the Church commands the imperatives of a living tradition, we neither go wrong in following the Church's lead nor fail in our responsibility in thinking things out for ourselves.

A point which in these days of liturgical controversy may easily be missed is that the liturgy is an *anamnesis*, a re-proposing of earlier assumptions and practices, a showing again of past rites in forms which makes them, age after age, contemporary. The liturgy is not something static and antiquarian, but is rather something dynamic, integrating, and everlastingly appropriate to its time. If liturgists recall the sacred signs of bygone ages it is only in order to mould them according to present conditions. The great thing is to make the Sabbath serve man—real, live, flesh-and-blood, contemporary man.

131

Biblical study, theological study, liturgical study, patristic study: all go together to make for the knowledge and service of God. But not all necessarily go together for the work of prayer. They should do, but they sometimes do not. Indeed they can sometimes be obstacles to prayer. Just as apologetics and controversy can lead to truth but as often as not lead to uncharity, so ecclesiastical studies can lead to prayer but as often as not lead to distraction and purely secular purposes.

The Church's influence on a particular generation or in a particular country will depend upon its inner life. Influence and prestige are one thing, inner life is another. Though ideally the two should go hand in hand, inner life tends to lag. Though ideally the two should go hand in hand, the concern is more often with the outward than the inward development. Since it is the Church's inner life and not its contemporary movements that we are interested in here, the spread of the faith is outside the scope of our subject. But as members of Christ's body we owe it to the Church to develop as far as we can the indirect apostolate of prayer and sacrifice.

The renewal which immediately involves us is personal renewal, self-renewal. In the measure that we achieve this we are helping in the ceaseless renewal of the Church. When we have got on with the work of renewing ourselves according to grace, we shall be ready to profit by the study of those things which relate, however remotely, to God. This is not to belittle ecclesiastical studies—quite the contrary—it is merely to warn against letting them extinguish the spark of prayer.

132

If study is to help the spiritual life it needs discipline and orientation. The same might be said of manual labour and the creative arts. Too great an eagerness, like too great a distaste, is harmful to recollection, and too great a preoccupation with the work for its own sake withdraws it from its destination in Christ. The work may be laudable, and the energy put into it may be edifying, but unless it promotes the Christ-life in the soul, it is, in the present context, wasted.

The connection will now be seen between the interior effort of the individual soul and the larger issue of the Church's growth. Why does the traditional New Testament standard fail to impress? Why are people cynical about the Christian ethic?

Why does Catholicism lack conviction to those outside? Certainly it is not because the gospel is out of date or because the Church has nothing more to give to the world. Surely it is because we who call ourselves followers of Christ have cut down Christ's teaching to the size of our own Christianity. It is because we have shaped the gospel instead of allowing ourselves to be shaped by it.

What Christ taught was not just something to be subscribed to, something superimposed upon life; it was something to be known from the inside and sweated out. As in the case of the liturgy, we have to have been *there*. Only will what we do for others be unmistakably Christlike when what is done inside ourselves is allowed to be done by Christ. When we have let Christ re-live his life in our lives we can forget about controversy and making converts: our apologetic is then his, and the souls who are drawn to the Church are drawn by him. All we have to concern ourselves with are prayer, penance, and example. We shall have quite enough to do looking after these.

133

One of the commonest mistakes is to imagine that our range of service is limited through a lack of opportunity. We see the fruitful work done by others and wonder why we have been less fortunately placed or less well equipped. But are we? Wherever we happen to be we are well placed for prayer, and whatever our natural limitations we are equipped for the supernatural life. We can leave the work of defining to the theologians. The Holy Spirit will see to it that there are always enough theologians in the Church to go round. We can leave the question of early usage to the liturgists and antiquarians: these too will not be lacking. Missioners? If God wants us on the mission field he will make the vocation clear to us, and in the meantime we can help the missions from where we are with our prayers and hidden lives.

So we do not have to be orators, broadcasters, television personalities, literary stylists, university lecturers, philosophers —or indeed experts in any branch of human endeavour—because what God wants of us before all else is that we be faithful to his will. And his will is as likely to be in none of these callings as in any of them. The only universal call is that of love.

You would think it to be so much easier to love and pray than to work your way to the top of a profession, but apparently, if numbers are anything to go by, this is not the case.

The vocation which covers all vocations is that of working with the Holy Spirit in the spread of Christ's gospel in the world. Whether this is done by preaching the word, by example, or by prayer will depend upon the individual grace, but this much is certain that without prayer and example the word can never be effectively preached. The gradual penetration of truth in an environment prejudiced by original sin and error is going on all the time, and though we know that the world must one day reach full stature in Christ we are meant to help in the process. Ultimately, whether we personally are faithful or not, truth will triumph. On the appointed day Christ will come again and bring all history to fulfilment. Until that day, each soul has his own small segment of history to account for.

134

Surveying the span of history we perhaps wonder whether creation was really worth it. So much sin, so much suffering, so much gone to waste, so much rejection of grace. Evidently it appears differently to God. The whole of time lies before him and had creation been not worth while, creation would not have happened. At the end of the world, the good will be made better and the bad will be dissolved. The parable of the wheat and the cockle: there is never any doubt about the ultimate harvest. The infinitely wise husbandman would not have bothered to sow if the only crop was going to be cockle. It is just that we, with our noses to the ground and seeing more of the cockle than the wheat, cannot project ourselves into the role of reaper.

Because life is everybody's business, the life of Christ as continued through the Christian centuries, and fragmented in different aspects and movements of the Church, is everybody's business too. It is probably the experience of all of us that while the life of Christ as revealed in the gospels elicits nothing but loving admiration, the same living reality as traced over nearly two thousand years elicits a quite different response. We can see Christ's life reproducing itself in the martyrs, in the poor and oppressed, in the unbroken tradition of sanctity, but we see also the worldiness and corruption in the Church, the intolerance and injustice, and find it hard to square the two. In his life on earth Christ did not advocate persecution of enemies, the accumulation of weath, ambition for power and position. He advocated the exact opposite. Yet in his life in the Church he has shown himself not indifferent to these things, and though the discrepancy must be apparent only and not real, it is enough to puzzle us.

Of course it is puzzling. Our Lord himself said it would be. He spoke about people being 'scandalised in me' and repeated again and again the need for faith. We know that where the Church has failed over the centuries it was not because Christ had failed but that the Church's members, being human, had failed. Leaders and subjects alike had turned their backs on Christ, so of course they debased his ideal.

135

Loyalty to the Church does not mean that we have to whitewash the actions taken by some of the Church's most prominent figures. Nor does it mean that we have to agree with the Church's policy on questions which have not to do with faith or morals. It means that whatever our natural dislike, whether its object is a personality or a policy, we do not set ourselves up as judges. If loyalty does not mean this, it cannot mean anything at all. I do not have to pretend that the Church is always right, but I do have to keep my mouth shut when I imagine the Church to be wrong.

I do not have to like what the Church tells me to do; I have to obey what the Church tells me to do. At the judgment I shall not be asked if I enjoyed the new regulations as regards the liturgy: I shall be asked if I fell in with them or opposed them. Liking or disliking does not signify. Faith and love signify, and if my love for Christ does not extend to accepting in faith the regulations which the Church sees fit to issue, then I have neither a true love for Christ nor the faith which sees his will in the rulings which come to me from Rome.

People talk about the interpretation of scripture, about the administration of sacraments, about the commandments of the Church as though the faithful have to be either unthinking machines on the one hand or possessed of a sixth sense on the other. Given faith, the Catholic is free of these alternatives. Faith puts no ban on thinking; nor does it endow with magical perception. Though faith is not a sixth sense, it does claim the right to lay down rules for the control of the other five. We obey with our bodies as well as with our wills; it is only our feelings and our judgments which remain our own. And even these, wayward and fallible and unpredictable though they are, come to heel eventually. Between them, the prayer of faith and the unopposed way of grace see to it that no part of the soul is left to stand apart.

136

As in the case of so much connected with bedrock religion, we do not have to possess special insights or skills to be obedient. We have to possess convictions. In order to be supernaturally obedient we have to believe in truths which are hidden from us. We have to take on faith the proposition that God wants us to serve him in a particular way, and according to rules laid down by himself. In inviting our complete submission, God asks for more than cold consent: he wants co-operation. In accepting the gospel challenge, we operate with Christ and in Christ. We enter into his activity, and his activity enters into us.

If we think of Christ's activity as taking place in the past tense, and as shared by us only in a figurative sense, we might just as well read the gospels as a collection of pious legends. If our understanding of the incarnation and redemption is limited to the knowledge that we can get heaven on Christ's merits, leaving out of account the part we can play in continuing his life and work on earth, we are not only missing the greatest opportunity open to man but are treating our inheritance as though it were some kind of trick. We are not *only* beneficiaries, legatees of the dead Christ; we are fellow workers in partnership with the living Christ.

Christ is the mediator, we are the redeemed. But though reclaimed by his act, we are not passive in our role of acceptance. We follow up our release from sin by accompanying him in his redemptive work. It is one of St Paul's most positive doctrines that those who share in his death share also in Christ's life after death, in his resurrection. His resurrection is ours by

99

anticipation. Easter is not only the feast of Christ's triumph; it is the herald of our own. What all of us would like of course would be to enjoy a sense of this sharing in Christ's resurrection, but because faith and hope are here the appropriate virtues we must be content with an assurance instead of a foretaste. We have to believe, without feeling it, that we are already living on a plane of existence which Christ has merited for us and which we can never fully appreciate in this life.

137

A right understanding of the resurrection, our own as well as our Lord's, should give depths to our view of human life as a whole and particularly to our view of the human body. The perfection to which we are destined in heaven is not the perfection of the angels but the perfection of human beings. It is all in the epistle to the Romans, chapters six and eight. 'If the spirit of him who raised Jesus from the dead dwells in you, then he who raised Christ Jesus from the dead will also bring to life your mortal bodies.' The reward of living in Christ on earth is living in Christ—and with the bodies which we possess on earth—in heaven.

Because we are baptised into the risen Christ we are destined ultimately to enjoy the same condition which he enjoys now, and since his body and soul are united so must ours be. St Paul sees the resurrection of the body as the logical consequence of baptism. The early practice of baptism by immersion brought out this idea in a way which is missed today. The Christian neophyte goes down into Christ's death and comes up in his resurrection. It is the same human organism throughout: the Christian does not shed his body in the water and emerge as a pure spirit. 'Buried with him by baptism' St Paul writes to the Colossians, 'you also rose with him by your faith in the power of God who raised him from the dead.'

If they could be made aware of the many implications of baptism, souls would gain enormously in their spiritual lives. For instance it is by baptism that we become incarnate in the body of Christ. The spirit of adoption which comes from the Father brings about the union of our human nature with the divine and human nature of the Son. The whole of us, body and soul, is made over to the whole of Christ. The person that is me is made one with the Person that is Christ. And if nothing but deliberate mortal sin can kill this relationship, the person that is me, flesh and all, must partake of the destiny which is Christ's. Christ's love which is the cause of my adoption is the cause also of the effect of my adoption. From his resurrection therefore derive both my adoption in baptism and my resurrection of which baptism is a pledge.

138

Only after the final judgment, when Christ has come again in glory, shall our bodies be reunited with our souls. In the meantime, assuming that we die in grace, we shall be perfectly happy but incomplete. It will be as souls and not as men that we shall enjoy our union with God. Not until we have got our bodies back shall we fully share in the glory of Christ's resurrection. When that stage is reached, when our senses are in harmony with our intellect, there will be no more changes for all eternity. God's act of bringing human nature into being will have justified itself. Only then, when body and soul are in complete agreement, will the last consequences of original sin be blotted out.

So closely does Christ's life resemble ours in all things save sin that there is an affinity even in this matter of waiting for the moment of glorification. The difference is that where Christ's glorification followed upon his resurrection, ours is long delayed. By denying himself the full use of his divine attributes while on earth, Christ chose to merit for himself the glory which was his by reason of his divine nature. When St Paul tells the Philippians that Christ 'made himself nothing by taking the nature of a slave, fashioned as he was in the likeness of men and recognised by outward appearance as man' he was showing how the Second Person of the Blessed Trinity divested himself of divine prerogatives with a view to meriting for man *and for himself* the resurrection and all that the resurrection was to stand for.

'We know that Christ, having risen from the dead, will die no more' St Paul explains to the Romans, 'death shall no longer have dominion over him.' Until he rose again from the dead, Christ chose that death *should* have dominion over him. This was so that he might share with man a common mortality. With man he placed himself *in via,* waiting for the final reunion of body and soul. Once death was conquered by the act of rising again, Christ restored to his human nature the privilege of immunity from death which was enjoyed by our first parents before the fall.

139

The necessary connection between Christ's resurrection and our own is made absolutely clear by St Paul when he tells the Romans: 'If this is what we proclaim, that Christ was raised from the dead, how can some of you say there is no resurrection of the dead? If there be no resurrection, then Christ was not raised. And if Christ was not raised then is our gospel null and void, and so is your faith . . . if Christ was not raised, your faith is of no account and you are still in your sins.' Having said this, St Paul abruptly points out the futility of living in an *un*resurrected Christ: at death they must find that all their Christian work was wasted. 'It follows that those who have died in Christ are utterly lost.'

'If it is for this life only that Christ has given us hope' is St Paul's conclusion, 'we are of all men most pitiable.' So the reason why the sacred writers, and later the fathers and theologians of the Church, have so much to say about the resurrection is that all our hope hinges on it. Without hope in an after life, there would be no point in faith, and only humanitarian reasons for charity. If our hope in an after life is verified by our faith in Christ's resurrection, we have not only a foundation on which to rest our service of God but also a promise which can draw us over the deserts of our despair.

'I am persuaded' wrote Thoreau, 'that fully two thirds of the world's population live out their lives in the condition of quiet despair.' This was written at a time when there was less to be despairing about, and if it was true then it is all the more true now. But in any case do people despair because of the state of the world? More often, and it is surely this that the writer has in mind, they see their own inner failure and quietly give up hope. Some of course are driven desperate by situations, and these are the ones who make a chaos of their lives, but the 'two thirds of the world's population' are those who sit in their own back gardens, who have given up.

140

Though the texts from St Paul already cited give grounds for hope in an ultimate happiness, and to this extent they must bring relief, there is no guarantee in St Paul or anywhere else that we shall find happiness on earth. Yet because we go on looking for it, and expecting it, we wonder what has gone wrong when we do not find it. The discrepancy between what we dreamed of in early life and what we are landed within later life affects us in one of two ways. Either we keep up our search and refuse to be disappointed, or we decide that it is not worth trying any more and so settle down to an unhappiness which we hope we shall be able to contain without disaster.

Clearly it is our Lord's intention that we should live positively, making use of what is provided for natural wellbeing. He has come that we should have life, and that our joy should be full. But there must always be some who, with the best will in the world, find nothing worth living for and whose joy is so intermittent as to be anything but full. Missing the import of the gospel and standing self-condemned, is there room for these in the scheme of God's service or must the best that they can hope for be to live out their time as unobstrusively as possible? It must be taken as axiomatic that there is always, whatever the person's temperament or condition of life, room in the service of God for everybody. Grace is not confined to the stereotypted, but is also given to misfits.

While there are many who have given up hope of finding happiness in this life there are few of these who do not sink into apathy and self-commiseration. Hopelessness is never without cause, and usually it can be traced to one of three deficiencies: lack of confidence either in God, in the future, or in oneself. If a man cannot trust in divine providence he will not be able to trust in much else, so the future can hold out little hope. The world, in looking for securities apart from divine providence, is disillusioned. But this is the world's business, and if the world wants it so, it has only itself to blame. Secularization, rationalism, materialism: these are not our concern. They bring their own punishment, and 'quiet despair' is part of it. Our concern is with the individual soul.

141

A man's want of confidence in the future and in himself can undermine the work of grace, depriving him of trust and bringing about an altogether false humility. There is the wrong kind of self-confidence which blusters along without a thought of God, and the right kind which claims no personal credit but undertakes whatever presents itself. The soul that relies more on God's grace than on natural ability can afford to be what is misleadingly called self-confident. People who do not expect to be happy, who have no confidence in their capacity for happiness, to a certain extent disqualify themselves from enjoying what God means them to enjoy. It is not God's fault when people do not develop their aptitudes.

A man's temporal happiness depends largely upon feeling that he is needed. He may not know it, but that does not matter. A man with no self-confidence never feels that he is needed. From this he concludes that he is not wanted and not loved. Under such conditions, even though he may avoid the evils of self-pity, it is difficult for him to look forward to anything, to do what he has to do with any sort of zest, to be in any positive sense happy. He is merely marking time, getting through another day, holding off despair. Naturally the man who feels he is occupying a certain space for a specified number of empty years will doubt if his existence is really justified. The best he can do is to conclude that unhappiness, even if it is not the normal state of man, is something which cannot be fought but which must be endured. This is perfectly true, as it happens, but it does not make for enjoyable living.

Once the reality of God's love, God's providence, God's promises is grasped, the lack of confidence in self and in the future no longer matter so much. Seen against its supernatural background, natural disappointment is insignificant. Indeed the sense of temporal emptiness may lead to the dawn of supernatural hope. A man directs his hopelessness to God, and discovers himself to be hopeless no longer.

142

Much of the spiritual life consists of beginning again after periodical defeats. Without the grace of hope it is impossible to turn one's failures into triumphs. The failures are occasions of learning the truth about oneself, and the triumphs are occasions of learning the truth about God's grace. 'He must increase and I must decrease . . . he has exalted the humble, and the rich he has sent empty away.' The light by which one sees oneself may be painful but it teaches humility. If it does not humble, it discourages, and the difference between humility and discouragement is not one of degree but of kind. Humility thrives on hope whereas discouragement thrives on the lack of it. The humble person, however crushed he feels by the weight of his failure, turns away from despair as instinctively as he turns away from pride and presumption. The discouraged person, if he takes his failure too much to heart, may well give in to despair.

It is the function of light to strengthen as well as to illumine. God does not show us ourselves without giving us the grace to do something about it. In seeing where we have gone wrong, we see also how we can begin again and go right. The uphill climb is not made any easier by the number of false starts which most of us make. But there is this for our consolation, that the willingness to start again counts for more in God's sight than the mistakes which we make in starting. If we were to be judged by our mistakes and not by our willingness it would be more virtuous to play for safety and attempt nothing. In everything that we do we risk failure, and if we did not the work would not be worth doing.

The principle of having to start again is laid down for us by our Lord in his discussion with Nicodemus. Nicodemus was managing on his own, getting along slowly, confident of salvation. Then at some point the light must have been granted him to see how insecure he really was and how it was necessary for him to seek out truth itself. Our Lord told him he had to be born again. As though it was a branding iron he accepted humility: from now on the weak man was made strong. Of all the minor characters in the gospel it is Nicodemus who gives the greatest encouragement to a weak man.

143

It is important to appreciate the connection between weakness, failure, and trust, because far more people in the world are weak, disappointed, and hesitant than strong, successful, and trusting. Distinctions must here be drawn. Because a man is disappointed with life it does not necessarily mean he is defeated by it. It is up to him to be defeated or not. Disappointment cannot invade the area which either consents to or resists defeat. God humiliates but he does not defeat. Even the devil does not defeat a man; all he can do is to put the occasion of defeat in man's way. The grace may not always be there to avoid disappointment, but it is always there to avoid defeat. The prevailing temptation for most people is to neglect this grace, and so to create a disposition towards defeat. All the devil has to do now is to remind the man of a failure or two, and the chances are that the man will defeat himself. This is real weakness, because this—and not the failure which may have been due to a number of causes—is giving in.

At every stage in the spiritual life the soul is faced with the question, in one form or another, of humiliation. Exteriorly or interiorly, something is bound to come along which either exposes or crushes, or both, and then the next stage will show whether the soul has taken a stand on grace or on self. Grace remains firm, self crumples up. The one goes to prayer, the other drops it; the one hopes all over again, the other gives weakness as the excuse for not trying; the one expands in charity, the other turns inwards and shrinks from being caught up in the affairs of men.

Ultimately, again as in the case of Nicodemus, it is a question of trust. Few have the courage to trust absolutely when they have been humiliated absolutely. It is so much easier to run away and hide. But hiding is found to be no answer. A man can hug his little misery to himself for a while, but he cannot survive in the wilderness alone. It is his lot to be cast with others, and with them to bear the marks of his shame. Even if he is a misfitting link he still belongs to the chain. Humiliation and charity go together.

144

Though mutual understanding is to be expected of our common vocation in the human family, mutual comprehension is not. If this distinction were more generally recognised there would be less loneliness in the world. But because the moment he gets into serious difficulties a man wants the freedom of another's mind, heart, and soul, he is doomed to disappointment. He finds himself alone in what he supposes to be an unfeeling world. It is not at all an unfeeling world. It is merely that this world, in contrast to the next, is peopled by men and women who have their own unique God-given lives to lead, and whose human limitations render them incapable of penetrating to the unique God-given identity of their fellows.

The idea of human identity precludes interpenetration. If we cannot comprehend Christ who is nearer to us in love than anyone whom we know on a natural plane, we cannot expect to comprehend, in the sense of being able to share at every level and in every articulation, our fellow creatures. The most we can do is to sympathise, try to understand, make allowances, show confidence. Not even the highest kind of love can get closer than this. And it is just as well that it cannot, because if mutual comprehension were possible in this life the element of faith and trust would be lacking. Faith and trust are as necessary to our human relationships as they are to our relationship with God. Because God for his part has no need for faith and trust in his dealings with his creatures, he can fully comprehend them. They have issued from his mind, deriving from him their continued existence. The link between us and our fellow creatures is very different.

What it means in practice is that the lonely, instead of pitying themselves for being unable to reach others, or be reached, must see individual lives as coalescing in the totality of the group. This, since the group is the body of Christ, is not as cold as it sounds. Where there are separate cells, even though they belong to an organism which lives by love, there are bound to be separate lonelinesses. Only Christ himself can come to the rescue here.

145

Conceding the separateness of the human personality, and the consequent inevitability of loneliness, we can nevertheless find crumbs of comfort in the way that God has kneaded us together. Human beings are not poured like grains of wheat into a sack. From our Lord's illustration of the leaven, repeated by St Paul, we can conclude that we are meant to form a loaf. Vertically, man relates to God with whom he aspires to union. Horizontally, man is related to man. At the horizontal level there must be union too. Confirmation of this can be seen in the way by which peace of soul, even happiness, follows altruism. Taking other people's troubles upon ourselves is invariably, whatever the cynics say, infinitely rewarding.

Furthermore it is a fact of experience that we do not really know ourselves until we know what is worrying other people. We grow in wisdom and the love of God to the degree that we grow in the loving knowledge of others.

What it amounts to is that each man has to stretch out and bring another, and another, and another, into his own private world with him as far as the nature of his species allows, and see each one as another whole human being for whom Christ died. A man has to make the most of his affinity both in nature and in grace. Charity does not happen automatically or by accident. Charity is the deliberate application of the super-natural motive to the natural instinct by which human beings want to live in harmony with one another. By communicating in the name of charity, a man serves God, his neighbour, and his own best interests. By denying his natural instinct and super-natural grace, a man may find a certain bitter satisfaction in his isolation but he will never find happiness. There is safety when God calls a soul to solitude, but only illusion and stag-nation when a soul chooses solitude because of the idea of it, and because association with others is found to be irksome. The would-be solitary must be sure that he wants God, and not merely that he does not want people.

146

Psychologists as well as spiritual directors are familiar with the kind of person who, knowing from experience under what conditions he is most himself, will throw away his chance of happiness by following a way of life which goes clean his true nature. In some people more than others, but perhaps to a certain extent in all, there exists a curious streak which works towards self-destruction. Falling short of perfection as aimed at, the will sets out to tear to bits the good which is within its capacity. If this meant only the waste of potential perfection and happiness it would be bad enough, but often the choice to gratify a jaundiced appetite can lead to anarchy against God. The soul prefers the acids of its discontent to the graces which are there for the asking, and in fighting against life the soul is, consciously or unconsciously, fighting against God.

Whatever the causes to which psychologists attribute this inversion, those who have come across it in the spiritual life will put it down quite simply to pride. But it is a form of pride which will need a more than ordinary grace to cure. If humility is to be the outcome, the soul must face doing exactly in reverse what was done before: where there was one kind of self-destruction there must now be another. In order to straighten out his life, the man who deluded himself in making his earlier decision must break down the false image he has made for himself and substitute a humbler one. It is his only way to happiness, let alone holiness.

All of which confirms the truth that man must leave himself flexible in God's hands. To pursue preconceived ideas in opposition to God's idea spells disaster. To allow the promptings of bitterness to dictate the terms of self-realisation can only realize a self which man should do all in his power to subdue. While the existence of this destructive self has to be recognized as part of the legacy of original sin, it need not become obsessive. The grace which has countered original sin can counter the perversities to which original sin makes mankind liable.

147

In some ways animals are more sensible than men. Of all animals it is only the lemming which shares with rational man the urge towards self-destruction. Lemmings, periodically stampeding in a seaward direction, devote themselves to mass suicide. While human beings are unreasonably preoccupied with weapons of wholesale annihilation, they do not normally go in for wiping out members of their own nation and tribe. But there is this parallel between people and lemmings that what the rodents do in the physical order human beings are inclined to do in the spiritual and moral order. A man tends to move with the herd, even when the herd is rushing headlong to destruction.

This is where the life of prayer should come to the rescue. Someone who prays, who is open to the unqualified operation of grace, is able to stand back from the stampede and consider by the light of the Holy Spirit the direction which the world is taking. 'What everyone else chooses to do' the soul of prayer can say, 'does not affect the one thing in the world which really matters to me . . . the only question I have to decide is how God wants me to act.' Unless the soul can say this and mean it, there is nothing to choose between him and the lemming.

In Walter Hilton's *Scale of Perfection* there is a famous passage which compares the soul on the way to God with a pilgrim on the way to Jerusalem. The pilgrim's face is set towards a definite destination, and since his desire is to give glory to God in the venture, he knows that attempts will be made to draw him away from his purpose. Though all the world may be moving in a different direction, may be coming to meet him, he must keep to his God-given course. He will be tempted to delay on the road, to branch off to right or left where he sees signs of habitation that attract him. He will get bored, he will wonder if he should ever have undertaken it, he will suspect the whole thing of being a delusion. But what the pilgrim knows all along is that he is sure of reaching his goal if only he remains faithful to prayer. In the long run it is our prayer which prevents us from becoming lemmings.

148

Without prayer a man is so much driftwood, at the mercy of the surrounding element. Even with prayer it is not easy to keep a straight course. The sad thing is when someone who has known prayer, and has persevered in it for a time, gives up. Such a soul is more adrift than one who has never taken it on because the direction which he once saw is now lost sight of. The other, the one who did not even begin to pray, had no direction anyway but that which his natural intelligence gave him. So the only way to stop drifting is to pray.

There are times in a person's life when, whether he values prayer or not, he feels utterly at sea. Nothing to hold on to, no help from people or books, a featureless horizon stretching to infinity. It is only God's grace which keeps the soul from sinking. But it is not enough merely to keep afloat and maintain the same position: there has to be movement, co-operation with the power of grace. Allowing the attraction, the soul can now increasingly respond. Prayer now becomes not so much a help to be drawn upon in an emergency but a habit whether it is felt to be a help or not. There is a change of outlook. The surrounding element, which, with its undertow, has been dragging at the soul, is seen now to be not such a menace after all. Whatever its threat at one time, the element is not alien but appropriate. Prayer has not changed the surrounding element, the created order (or if you like to call it 'the world'), but has changed the soul's view of it. Prayer has given to the soul something of God's view of it, so that the natural is shown to be capable of a supernatural interpretation.

In the perspective of faith, everything that is can be viewed as belonging to love and truth. It is not that creation suddenly takes on the appearance of loveliness—as if by a piece of trick lighting—but that all temporal reality is related to eternal reality, and all relative good is valued in the light of absolute good. The soul knows, without being told, that God is absolute goodness, truth, and beauty.

149

The desire to go back on the spiritual commitment may come from natural restlessness (and usually does), but it may also come from a genuine but mistaken belief that the supernatural cause would be better served by exterior rather than by interior works. Taking human instability first as the cause of secession, we must recognize it as a serious weakness of character and not merely dismiss it as a harmless trait. The experimenting, questing, foot-loose spirit is one which, if it is detrimental to any sort of work, is particularly detrimental to the kinds of work which do not show. Boredom with routine, impatience to see quick results, frank desire for change: on any showing self-discipline is called for here. You should not need religion to tell you that steadfastness is a virtue.

If fixity of purpose is to be aimed at in everyday life it is all the more necessary in the spiritual life. One of the main obstacles to constancy in any sort of life is wistfully dreaming of another sort of life. Though we are always being told that dreams are no substitute for concrete duties, most of us waste time and opportunity imagining ourselves magnificently controlling hypothetical situations. Our lives would run more smoothly if we did not have grand ideas about ourselves. Indeed if, beyond directing ourselves towards God, we had no ideas about ourselves at all. The virtues of the saints are the self-forgetting virtues. The trouble is that modern civilization, psychology, literature, medicine, education and religion are bent upon self-questioning. Motives, ends, and means are multiplied, labelled, card-indexed, produced as evidence. Only what can be filed is thought to be of value. But the one thing which really matters is love, and this defies classification.

Love, if only it is allowed to, settles such questions as appropriate environment, congenial activity, conflicting loyalties, human rights, justice and equity. Love, on the Christian principle, solves everything. But because man wants so many things besides love, and refuses to employ his potentialities in the service of love, he becomes increasingly restless, greedy and analytical.

150

When asked what he considered to be the most exacting aspect of the religious life, a certain experienced superior replied without a moment's hesitation: 'Staying on the job'. This can be taken to apply to the spiritual as well as to the monastic life. It signifies more than the determination not to bolt. Though it bears first upon obedience and perseverance, staying on the job knows such refinements as patience in the face of panic, endurance of doubt, silent submission when misjudged, suppression of criticism and ambition, continuance in the drudgery of uncongenial and unrewarding work, seeing no hope of relief and refusing to ask for it, the fight against resentment and self-pity, the rejection of material compensations. If staying on the job demands a measure of heroism, it certainly demands a resolute unselfishness. Even in those who are not (for want of a better term) imaginative, and to whom routine occupations are no great burden, the spirit of rebellion will assert itself occasionally, and there will be a longing for rest, change, or sheer oblivion.

There must be very few people in the world who positively *like* monotony. Yet because so much of life is drearily monotonous, those who are looking to serve God with their lives must accustom themselves to dull steady daily labours, and make of them an acceptable sacrifice. This can be done effectively only by staying with the interior job of prayer. It is stability in prayer which brings order and stability to outward occupations. Prayer is no more exciting than shelling peas, but fidelity to the one kind of grace makes another kind of grace look after the outward work.

It is hard to see how, without a life of prayer to support him, anyone can maintain an even pressure indefinitely without complaining or asking to be relieved. Interior prayer, if not absolutely guaranteeing external steadfastness, at least disposes the soul for the grace of fortitude. Fortitude begins on the inside before it merits recognition for services rendered. Perhaps we think of fortitude too much in terms of heroic acts and not enough in terms of staying on the job.

151

'Fortitude', 'steadfastness'. Something old-fashioned about them? Not to the psalmist whom most would agree to be timeless. The psalter opens with a comparison suggesting firmness, stability, permanence: the sinner is blown about like dust over the face of the earth, but the just man is planted like a tree which strikes roots. The idea is repeated in the seventy-ninth psalm where the soul prays to the Lord that the planting may be confirmed and that no enemy may be allowed to scatter the branches or loosen the roots. Again the soul prays that a settled home may be found in the house of the Lord: 'that I may dwell in the house of the Lord all the days of my life.' The Messias is described as the foundation stone which may not be moved, and the 'stone which is become the head of the corner'. It is always the sinner who wanders about seeking his pleasure and not finding it.

In the New Testament we are also exhorted to steadfastness. Our Lord tells us to *abide* in him, not merely experiment in his life. He that perseveres to the end, this man shall be saved. 'Because you have *continued* with me' you inherit my promises. And in the first chapter of St James: 'he that wavers is like a wave of the sea which is moved and carried about by the wind . . . a double minded man is inconstant in all his ways.' 'Take heed' says St Peter, 'lest being led aside by the error of the unwise, you fall from your own steadfastness.'

Surely it is because we are so restless, internally as well as externally, that we make little headway in prayer. Wanderers, nomads, we find it hard to settle before God in prayer. The imagination, given too much freedom outside prayer time, keeps on straying when the will is trying to rope in all the faculties and direct them towards God. The memory gets busy, and rebels against the spirit. Emotions refuse to be tied. 'Free yourself' the psalmist says in the Lord's name, 'and see that I am God.' Empty your mind of the images which jostle one another, because only then can you come to the clear steady vision of me.

152

It is a pity that Catholics do not make more use of the psalter in their prayer. You seldom hear of anyone drawing upon the psalms for inspiration; more often it is the meditation book or certain indulgenced prayers. Because the psalmist was an intensely human person, expressing a wide range of human emotions, what he wrote should be of interest to everyone. Our moods are seen reflected in his moods, and there can surely be no experience of ours—whether of joy, failure, hope, resentment, panic, love, disappointment, faith, puzzlement, anger, humility, desire for an end to everything—which has not been experienced by him.

The psalter is not just Hebrew poetry, an archaic literary form, material for the printing of breviaries. Nor, on the other hand, does the psalter work magic. Divinely inspired, the psalms meet us at our human level and translate our activity to a supernatural dimension. With practice we come to find our spirituality shaped by the psalms and reflecting their spirt. When at a loss during set times of prayer we shall find ourselves instinctively groping about for an appropriate verse, and outside the times of prayer we shall find ourselves using phrases from the psalms as aspirations. Certain psalms will come to have a special appeal, certain passages will have associations, even certain words will carry a power of their own.

In case it might be thought that such a use of the psalms must have the same cramping effect as the slavish use of the meditation book, and so defeat the main purpose, we can remind ourselves that our Lord was reciting the twenty-first psalm as he was dying on the cross. Indeed the messianic psalms give us as deep an insight into the sacred humanity as any of the prophetical writings in the Old Testament. Even Isaias and Zacharias, though giving more in the way of signs by which the Messias may be recognised, bring us no closer than do the psalms to the mind and heart of Christ. The psalter is not only the word preparing for the coming of the Word, but also the word which reiterates the echo of his death.

153

If we thought of the psalms more as personal expressions and aspirations, and less as verses to be recited in public, we would find them more helpful. In contemplating the psalms, as distinct from rattling them off, we learn more about the attributes of God than we are likely to learn from a theological treatise. Divine mercy is the running theme, but there is also much to be learned of divine power, holiness, wisdom and justice. Corresponding to God's patience with sinners is the cry of the afflicted soul begging for pardon and attention. Time and again the soul laments the withdrawal of God's protecting hand, only to find in the end that his hand has been there all along.

When, leaving aside the psalter for a more wordless prayer, the soul is moved by the same sentiments that moved the psalmist—trust, compunction, praise, gratitude—the presumption is that the soul is in the right way. But there is just this to be noted, that the psalmist's self-reproach can too easily become, with us who are today more introspective, sulks. There is perhaps this to be noted too, that the psalmist's bewilderment at God's apparent indifference can become, in us, a nagging bitterness. Prayer is not spoiled by distractions to anything like the extent that it is spoiled by the resignation which has gone sour.

If there are passages in the psalms which suggest querulous complaint, these are more than balanced by the acts of trust which in almost every case immediately follow. In our own dealings with God there is danger that the acts of trust do not so immediately follow. Every prayer, however brief, should contain, if only by implication, the element of trust. As prayer springs from love and finds its term in love, so it must move by the way of trust or it will never move at all. In the next life the prayer which we shall offer to God will be different: it will be all love. The trust which we have had to exercise on earth will be verified. In the meantime the more there is of trust in our prayer the more there is also of love.

154

It is a curious thing that priests and religious whose daily vocal prayer is largely composed of the psalms derive their spirituality mostly from other sources. You would suppose that their thinking would be influenced by the imagery and expression of what they read at intervals throughout the day. But this is rarely found to be the case. Perhaps readers of the psalms unconsciously allow too much to the loss suffered in a series of translations. Perhaps they attach too much importance to references which today sound anachronistic, to a civilization and topography very different from what we know. But why bother about these accidentals when the essential content is that of love, praise, penitence of heart? The psalter was not composed primarily as a book of poetry but as a book of prayer.

Asked what line of the psalms he would choose as being most representative of the spirit of the psalter, a man who had been reciting the psalms for many years cited the opening words of the twenty-second psalm: 'The Lord rules me and I shall want for nothing.' This might stand for the attitude of mind most conducive to the action of grace. It is the condition which Christ wants to see in his disciples when he says in the Sermon on the Mount: 'Be not solicitous for your life, what you shall eat; nor for your body, what you shall put on . . . after all these things the heathens seek . . . your Father knows you have need of these things.'

Worries are disposed of only by confidence in God's love. If we look at the causes of our worry we may be able to do something towards lessening them, but even when we have eliminated one source of worry there are a hundred others waiting to take its place. Far better to look more at the promises of God than at the causes of anxiety. The very act of handing over our personal weakness and insufficiency to God brings its measure of peace. When we know our problems to be insoluble we are safe: God will then either solve them for us or give us the grace to go on living with them unsolved.

155

Useless worry not only comes between us and God but also

between us and other people. A familiar figure is the kind of religious person who is so concerned about himself, about his sins, about his difficulties that he has no concern left over for others. The responsibility owed by the soul of prayer to souls of the more active life is not wholly fulfilled by praying for the human race. How to strike the balance between what is given directly to God in prayer and what is given indirectly by seeing to people's needs is an ever open issue. The argument will always go on, and no conclusion brings satisfaction. But at least it is certain that we may not (particularly now since the Second Vatican Council) wrap ourselves up in our recollection and refuse to look out upon the contemporary world. While trying to live in the city of God, we are also living in the city of man.

Many devout souls suffer a curious inhibition where it is a question of helping others. Feeling that they can do so little, they are content to do nothing. Nothingness may not be canonized, and the fear of over-activity does not justify inaction. It would be nearer to charity to do too much for others than to turn one's back, in the name of a higher charity, on charitable activity.

Activity can be divided into three kinds: instinctive, intelligent, inspired by grace. The instinctive or sensitive kind we share with animals, and though planted in us by God for our completeness, these physical impulses are, until the will comes in to give them direction, morally neutral. Yawning when tired, feeling afraid when about to be run over in the street, wanting a place near the fire on a cold day: these are automatic reactions and do not of themselves affect the life of prayer. When man acts as man, using his intelligence, he acts morally or immorally according to the use he makes of his rational nature. He may be swayed by his sensitive and animal qualities, but his life is lived at a rational level. From the natural point of view man's relations with man are part instinctive and part rational. From the supernatural point of view they are conducted in charity. It is this activity, namely love of others in Christ, which concerns us.

156

When rational man is moved by grace to perform an act of religion he is living at the highest level of his nature. Even in order to perform a work prompted by instinct or intellect he need's God's help—because without God's help he cannot keep alive—but when he acts according to grace he is drawing upon a new force. Instinctive and reasoning acts are natural to him: prayerful and charitable acts are supernatural. It is a mistake to think of the supernatural factor only in connection with mystical states and extraordinary gifts: we are drawing upon the supernatural every time we practise a virtue or say a prayer.

Most of us would have to admit that we live more at the instinctual and rational level than at the supernatural level. This is a great pity and a great waste. What grace enables us to do is to mount from the automatic response to the considered response, and then from the considered response to the response of faith and love. The whole of our training in the spirit amounts to nothing else but the gradual passing from the natural to the supernatural, from feeling to faith. If the process took time in the case of the apostles ('how long a time have you been with me, Philip, and you have not known me?') it is not surprising that the principle works slowly with us.

All this has been leading up to the need, unrecognised by some and belittled by others, to supernaturalise our every activity, and in particular the activity of love. Love plays such a large part in our lives as human beings that as Christians we must see to its supernatural relevance. Without the supernatural to steer it along its proper course, love can lose itself in any number of back alleys. This is where the prayer life should be of inestimable value, imposing sanctions on the negative side and on the positive side pointing to ideals. Character alone is not likely to be strong enough to control the emotional side of human effection, but where the will is informed by grace a new character is at work which looks to the source and end of love, at love's essential, before it considers love's pleasureable expressions.

157

Souls who are attracted to the interior life are as anxious to be successful as everyone else, but they tend to identify success with a particular kind of interior perfection. True success is measured by the harmony existing between exterior and interior activity. It is a mistake to look upon love, the fulfilment of the law, as exclusively the love of God. The law is fulfilled only when we go on from the love of God to the love of our fellow human beings. It has always been the tendency on the part of the devout to form an image of God which is so personal and intimate as to leave out of account his human reflections—people. Many of us love Christ but would far prefer it if there were not so many other cells in his mystical body.

But Christ is just as much in the importunate visitor, in the tiresome correspondent, in the noisy child, in the tradesman and the tax-collector and the man who looks over my shoulder to read my paper in the subway as he is in me. These people are my brothers in Christ, and if I miss seeing Christ in them I shall miss seeing Christ in myself. It is not for me to call anyone an outcast. In fact it is particularly to those who are cast out that my love must be extended. If I am following in the footsteps of Christ, my mission is to publicans and sinners. He himself said that 'they that are well have no need of a physician but they that are sick.'

Another thing which many interior souls are slow to understand is that a human being—not a saint, it should be noted, but a human being—cannot achieve self-fulfillment apart from his fellows. The effort to get on with others is not an act of supererogation which can be dispensed without harm to rational completeness (as would be for instance prison-visiting or belonging to a welfare club) but is a necessity. A man, as a man, needs to go out from himself into the lives and minds of others. The social unit to which man belongs is not just his family and circle of friends; it is mankind.

158

Not only is there a law in our members which wars against the spirit and tempts to sin, but there is a law too which appears to be on the side of the spirit but which in fact wars against it. This is the law in us which tempts to personal autonomy. Pleading detachment from human affection and the avoidance of distraction, this spurious law is the enemy of the one thing, namely individual wholeness, which it claims to be preserving. We are whole only when we are one with everyone else. This unity of outlook has to be universal in application, because by being selective it fails in an essential quality.

Christ died for all, and not merely for an elect percentage

of mankind. 'When you give a dinner or a supper' he said, 'call not your friends, your brethren, your kinsmen, nor your neighbours who are rich, lest a recompense be made and they invite you back. But when you make a feast, call the poor, the maimed, the lame and the blind. And you shall be blessed because they have not wherewith to make you recompense. Recompense shall be made you at the resurrection of the just.' This is one of the texts on which we Christians make a poor showing, but even if we are not generous enough to take it literally we can at least apply the principle—which is to a universal charity.

So we must be on our guard against this temptation which disguises itself as a grace: the instinct which shrinks from closeness to our fellow human beings. Physchologists have one name for it, theologians another. By refusing to break down the barriers and by clinging to our independence we are not only being proud and uncharitable but are also defying the law of our nature—and a good law this time, not the kind of fallen law which tempts. Whatever the call to contemplation, it can never be the call of grace to contract out from mankind and live on a lonely peak. Somehow an exchange must be assured which means more than mutual toleration. It means welcome, consideration, the crossing over from self to another self. This is why Christianity, the law of love, alone of all religions brings completeness to man.

159

It is one thing to claim universal benevolence and another to go out of one's way to express it. In the sense that we cannot help getting caught up in other people's affairs, however distantly, social involvement is passive. Whether passive involvement is resented or enjoyed, it is something which we allow for because it happens to us and we always allow for the inevitable. But while active involvement is not always inevitable, it is something which, as followers of Christ, we must not only allow for but enter into with a good grace. It is our supreme opportunity of showing that we are in fact followers of Christ.

Quite as difficult as getting near to other people in charity is letting them get near to us. Either we are shy, or have a bad manner, or show that we have not much time, or are afraid of being committed to a prolonged heart-to-heart relationship, or suspect that we shall be laughed at, or misunderstood, or misquoted. So in the end, rather than expose ourselves to innumerable hazards, we feel that the easiest thing is to keep people at bay. We become accordingly inaccessible except on our own terms, dismissive to all but those whom we have chosen for friendship. The idea of universality is now quite lost, and what we like to think of as charity is nothing but a purely natural selectiveness.

Often when we are with people we are only half present to them. Having admitted to ourselves that we are not interested in them, or in anything they may have to say, we mentally wander off. Physically we are there, nodding and smiling, but our charity is miles away. We think it will not be noticed if we withhold our attention (perhaps we can be praying instead), and though at the conscious level this may be so, unconsciously the other person comes up against an obstacle and is not encouraged to go on. Charity is demanding, has need of great patience, may never surrender to mood, must forswear the compensation of telling a third party afterwards how uncongenial the person was to whom the kindness was extended. A martyred charity may be edifying after a fashion, but it is not likely to win much supernatural reward.

160

Just as charity is not necessarily giving people money, so it is not necessarily giving people advice. More often it consists in listening while other people give you or themselves advice. Some people do not expect an answer when they talk, but they do expect you to listen. Listening can be the greatest penance but it can also be the greatest charity. If listening is looked upon chiefly as a penance it will not do much in the way of charity. There are those who like to argue in conversation— not so as to reach a conclusion or to defeat you, but simply because it amuses them—and here there is no obligation in charity to humour them. There are enough arguments in the world without adding to them when they are a luxury.

In order to communicate charity you do not have to flatter, pose, exchange secrets, pretend to an intimate knowledge which you do not possess, kindle emotion or be a mine of information. You have to try to be in sympathy, you have to make the other person's concerns more important than your own. Our Lord could not have made clearer the practical aspect of charity: do for others what you would like others to do for you. The golden rule has been repeated so soften that it has ceased to speak. Yet if you take the golden rule seriously, you will see how it not only excludes all insincerity—nobody wants to be lied to—but on occasion calls for the administration of stern measures. Since you should want to be corrected of your faults, you should look upon it as an act of charity when you have to correct other people's.

If you are placed on earth with a mandate from God to help others as well as yourself to self-fulfillment, to perfection in fact, then it must be your duty to study how best another's soul may profit by association with you. How many of us do this? Do we not get out of our responsibility on the grounds that we are not worthy to preach, and that it would be the height of arrogance to believe that others should benefit by coming in touch with us. 'Am I my brother's keeper?' Yes, as a matter of fact you are.

161

The Church is not just a social organization with religious responsibilities. It is not even a religious society from which its members may expect certain benefits. It is essentially a household which sustains itself on, and exists to promote, love. The fact that its members must believe certain doctrines, must obey certain rules, must accept certain sacramental ministrations on pain of excommunication: this is not the primary consideration of the Church. The primary consideration is the development of charity in the human soul. This means that we, the members of Christ's Church, are not linked together because we happen to agree in our allegiance. While sharing a common belief, we justify our life in Christ by trying to understand one another, by considering the needs of one another, by going out in love to one another.

It is accordingly a good thing to examine ourselves on a text in Galatians where St Paul exhorts us to 'practise generosity to all, and above all to those who are of one family with us in the faith'. Belonging to one family we owe one another more than a detached benevolence; whether we like it or not we are committed to one another, and the only way in which we can justify our place in the Christian family is by supporting one another as St Paul says with 'generosity to all'. If our generosity stops short at people who annoy us, we have just as truly missed the point of our life in Christ as if our generosity stopped short at a Church's command or a Church's doctrine.

If we cannot bring ourselves to love those who are opposed to us, if we operate simply as a Christian study group, if we push the fetish of privacy so that nobody is allowed to break in upon our recollection, we have got Christianity wrong and the prayer life wrong. We are called upon, particularly at this time of dawning ecumenism, to open the doors of the Church and of our own souls. For too long we have kept the doors, if not tight shut, at least on a chain. We have to meet people sympathetically—people who, whether Catholics or not, find the Church uncongenial—because only on such a basis can we fulfil St Paul's exhortation, and practise love.

162

'All power is given to me in heaven and in earth. Going therefore teach ye all nations.' (The New English Bible has: 'Full authority in heaven and on earth has been committed to me. Go forth therefore and make all nations my disciples.') These were our Lord's words immediately before he ascended into heaven. In the first sentence he was stating in the most solemn way possible his right to command, his right over men's lives. In the second sentence he made use of this right. He was not commanding the apostle only; he was equally commanding the man of prayer. The difference between the missioner and the man of prayer is not one of kind. The vocation to prayer and to an apostolate is the same: it is merely a question of the missioner using one means and the man of prayer another. Even the means to some extent coincide: the missioner has to pray or his work for souls will falter; the man of prayer must work for souls or his prayer will falter.

Far from absolving the man of prayer from the apostolate —and even some sort of outward apostolate—the interior life commits him to it. He must show by the measure of his charity that there is not one truth for the catechism and another for contemplation. 'I am the way and the truth and the life.' The truth is undivided. Exactly how Christ, the truth, is to be furthered by the individual so that it reaches all nations is not laid down. Some are called to preach it by word of mouth, some by writing about it; all by example in social contact. This much is certain, that given the goodwill, the follower of Christ will find, whatever his state of life, occasions for pressing the cause of Christ.

If it is objected that no sooner do opportunities of practising the apostolate appear than they melt away again, it must be pointed out that the providence of God knows what it is about. The apostle is a go-between, a line of communication, and for long as the zeal for souls and the desire to communicate charity is present, the line is kept open and is presumably, though in a way known only to God who has so arranged it, in use. The good to be communicated is his after all, not ours. God cares for his own—in his way.

163

Though God wants our co-operation, and this is what we have come into the world to give, he is not tied to it. The sunrise does not wait upon the cock crowing. If we withhold our co-operation it will be our loss, but not his. As St Ignatius is so emphatic in declaring, God has no need of us and it is simply out of his goodness that we are able to return his love. He loves us with an infinite love, but he can go on being God without us. It is difficult for us, with our knowledge of love limited to human affection reciprocated at its own natural level, to imagine a divine love which can continue in its own eternal happiness while at the same time spurned by an object of his love, by an object which he himself has created out of love. Yet unless we claim the power to make God miserable, such must be the case.

The language of devotion is misleading here. A piety which is not founded on theological fact may stir the emotions but cannot advance the soul towards truth. Truth is not only more important than sentiment but in the long run far more useful to the work which piety is aiming to foster—namely prayer and the service of God. The idea that God can be hurt when we commit sin, the idea that his love for us changes when we sin, the idea that he must be propitiated if his anger is to cool after our sin before we can restore the relationship: these are only some of the misconceptions to which the extravagant phraseology of devotional literature can give rise.

An understanding of God's immutability should not only clear up false notions about how he deals with souls but also prove enormously encouraging in the life of prayer and trust. Our sins and their consequences are not minimised by the knowledge that God does not change—the fact that Christ suffered because of our sins is evidence enough of our guilt and of the hurt inflicted—but at lease we have the comfort of knowing that Christ reigns now in glory, and that no change or shadow of alteration can come about to lessen the infinity of divine happiness.

164

When we talk about 'pleasing God' we do not mean that God enjoys a sense of pleasure as the result of our action, still less that he reacts to our act with gratified surprise. Though they are clear about what the term does not mean, theologians are not so clear about what it does. Nor can the theologians be blamed for this since, in the words of scripture itself, 'no man has known the mind of the Lord' and 'incomprehensible are his ways'. This much anyway is certain that the eternal mind of God is not subject to emotional variations, and that therefore when we please God we are not producing the same kind of effect as we do when we please people. What we do when we respond to his grace, and this can be said without qualification, is to assert his glory.

But, it might be objected, God already possesses the fulness of glory, so what is the point of trying to add to it? The answer is that we do not *add* anything to God by rendering him our service, but in using our free will in the way that God gives us the grace to use it we are uniting our human will with his. We are reflecting him at the highest level of our being, and in this way are 'partaking of his glory' while still living in this flesh.

Much of our vanity in the spiritual life (though a better term than 'vanity' is the oldfashioned one, 'vain glory') comes of imagining that in our service we are conferring some benefit on God. We should think of it from the other way round: every act of service which we perform is a benefit conferred by God upon *us*. Whatever we manage to do for God we still remain, our Lord says, 'unprofitable servants'. Our role is a very humble one indeed, and the more sincerely we acknowledge this the more likelihood there is that God will make use of us to reflect his glory. Always we have to bear in mind that by the right use of our free will we are choosing and loving one who has first chosen and loved us. From all eternity he has chosen and loved us. There is nothing new that we can give in time. But what we *can* do is to respond in time to the choice and love which exists in eternity.

165

It is best to think of God's relationship with man as love eliciting love. Thought of in this way there is less emphasis on what I am doing for God, and more on what God is doing in me. It is as though God were a blood donor who gets his own blood back. (This is a very imperfect simile because it suggests that God has to be deprived of something before he can expect a return. God's love, being infinite, cannot be either weakened in the giving or strengthened in the receiving.) The point in all this is that the love with which God loves us can, if we let it, take us away from our fallen selves and into the orbit of love itself.

So from our point of view we can either focus the power to love upon ourselves, and come to a dead end, or else focus it outside ourselves upon God, and so go on to develop it indefinitely. Whichever way you look at it our whole life centres round love, and sooner or later we have to decide which way it shall go. If love were not the most important thing about life, the world would not concern itself as much as it does about one aspect of it, nor would the gospel concern itself as much as it does about the other. All sin is loving wrong, and all virtue is loving right. Love is the fulfilment of the law, and, in reverse, the repudiation of it.

What this amounts to is that all humanly expressed charity, whether considered in relation to neighbour or in relation to God, is possessed by favour of charity itself and in virtue of the fact that God has taken the soul with him into a partnership of love. Since it is that which makes the Persons of the Blessed Trinity one, divine charity can be said to constitute the eternal life of God, and since it is the source of God's love for man it cannot but anticipate man's love for God. Charity in man, as St Bernard points out, is not a human experiment or speculation: it is a divine reality—more, it is a being. This being is therefore the starting point of man's charitable activity. It should not be surprising, and certainly should be very heartening, that man, created in the image and likeness of God, is able to do what God himself does. He can, by his co-operation, continue the work of love within himself and in the world.

166

'He has set in order charity within me.' This line from the Canticles prompted St Bernard to explain at some length both the subject of charity in general and in particular the 'ordering' of charity within the soul. By the ordering of love, and under the direction of grace, the soul returns to its true nature from which it had departed by the wrong use of love. The ordering of love is for St Bernard, then, a conversion, a re-alignment with its source and principle—God. For St Bernard it means a 'purification', a 'convalescence', by which the interior movement of love expresses itself exteriorly.

None of this would be very practical were it not that it closely affects the way we pray. In saying that 'the soul, already like the Word by nature, shows itself to be also like him in will when it loves as it is loved' St Bernard was speaking of the soul in prayer as much of the soul in the activity of love. If, on St Bernard's theory, the ordering of charity in the soul constitutes a return, as far as is possible in this life, to the pre-fall state of man, then the conversion is to an integrity in which prayer becomes second nature. Though the human faculties and appetites cannot be wholly freed from the effects of original sin, they can be made to operate more in accordance with their original design; they can further rather than hinder the activity of charity.

By the same token human beings can never, except in the case of Mary whose immaculate conception secured it for her, pray with the purity of our first parents before the fall. Nevertheless St Bernard's 'purification' and 'conversion' can be seen as strengthening our nature, and therefore as bringing us to resemble more closely the likeness of God. Had original sin done away with the possibility that the human soul should in some way resemble and reflect God, there would be no point in praying or in trying to practise charity. But because there is an analogy between man and God—what little we know of the divine nature is derived from what we know of human nature—the 'ordering of charity within us' brings out the image and likeness. Sin overlays the likeness, but the potentiality remains.

167

With charity ordered within us, and with the likeness which we bear to God reconditioned, the life of prayer is not only made more immediate but more manageable and habitual. Love and prayer run parallel, so that the soul without love does not pray and the soul that is wholly animated by love prays incessantly. The element of self-seeking in love is reflected in the element of self-seeking in prayer. All we have to do to dispose ourselves for the ordering of charity within us is to simplify and unify. We do not have to go in for extraordinary displays of devotion or break our previous records for time spent on our knees. As regards everyday life the problem of how we shall mount from egotistic love and prayer to a purer expression is not so much our problem as God's, and for the main work we have to wait upon his grace. This is what St Bernard, in his discussion of the right order, takes for granted.

It is a relatively modern habit to ask of the spiritual life 'What do I have to do next?' In the older view it is assumed that if we do what we can now, we can safely leave it to God to take the next step for us. Belonging as we do to an era of experiment, formula, and deduction from statistics, we tend to reduce the spiritual life to an exact science and to hanker after a system which can be checked. But problems of the spirit, whether they are to do with principle or practice, cannot be fed into a computer. Perplexities have to be resolved not by the law of averages, or even by accredited precedent, but by practising from moment to moment what grace is giving us to practise. By practising charity and prayer.

There must always be perplexities and crises in the spiritual life. Without them there would be no room for faith and de-pendence upon grace. Doubts, alarms, emergencies: these things are not inimical to the life of prayer. Religion in general, and in particular its interior manifestation, must necessarily make people aware of anomalies, dangers, subtleties, exigen-cies, which would escape the notice of the worldly or irreligious.

168

Souls would be spared much disappointment and unnecessary heartsearching if they could be brought to recognise as integral to the spiritual life the existence of tensions. The soul has to accept the role of battleground, most of which is jungle, over which opposing pressures wage unceasing war. This should not discourage; it should stimulate. The knowledge that God's grace is always at hand, that it is never more at hand than when the difficulties are greatest, should at any rate take the nervous sting out of the situation. Tension need not be nervous tension, and pressures have no power of themselves to obsess. Since man is not created to drift placidly along his course, the crises which come up in his life are to be allowed for as belonging necessarily to his journey.

We are so anxious to follow the way as it is printed on the map that when we lose track we imagine we have lost everything. But why should we expect to be able to trace our progress mile by mile? Our Lord never said that this was necessary. He did not tell us that we had to be sure about *our* way but about his. 'I am the way' he said. 'Walk while you have the light' and then he warned us that the light would go out. We have only to read the first chapter of St John to see that what is wanted of us is not self-determination, self-propulsion, but acknowledgement of Christ's claim, and trust in his power to verify it.

Jeremias laments that the Lord has shut up his ways with square stones and turned his paths upside down, that the Lord has set him in dark places and has made him desolate. Ezechiel tells how Jerusalem has to be cast into the fire, reduced to ashes, rendered unfit for any work. Isaias describes God's people as given over for spoil, as wasted and burning, as struggling in deep waters. The psalmist is constantly crying out about having lost his way in the wilderness, and only rarely does he admit that the Lord has shown him where to go. The point of these outbursts of complaint is that in every case the soul is attributing the loss of light and direction to the agency of the Lord . . . from whom ultimately the rescue is expected.

169

The difficulties experienced by interior souls are amply

compensated for when it is understood that God uses human affliction as the raw material of love. 'In his wisdom God wills man to be tried by tribulation so that when man fails and God must come to his rescue' says St Bernard in his treatise on love, 'God may receive honour from man.' The trials which God sends us are accordingly to be seen not so much as tests of our strength—we have little enough strength even when at our best —as invitations to our love. 'God makes all good things only that they may be turned to his love' says St Bernard again, and among the 'good things' he would rank suffering as one of the best. If the external works of God's creation give glory to their Creator by merely being what they are meant to be, then the works which touch man's interior life, because they can be diverted from their purpose by a selfish choice, are of greater worth and give greater glory. Suffering, received with love and directed towards God with love, is such a work.

While it is easy to see how it must give glory to God when we love his works, whether external as in nature or internal as in spiritual trials and desolations, for his sake, it is not so easy to see how we can give glory to God by loving ourselves for his sake. Have we not learned that the love of self is responsible for all our troubles? St Bernard felt exactly this but he discovered the answer. 'I hated my soul, as I would still do had not he who first loved it granted me also some beginning of love for it.' Not only are the two loves, love of self and love of God, reconciled, but the lesser love ministers to the greater.

That this doctrine of St Bernard's about loving oneself for God's sake is neither an intellectual trick nor an oratorical fancy can be seen by the support which it gets from the word of God. 'Have pity on your own soul, pleasing God' we read in the thirtieth chapter of Ecclesiasticus, 'gather up your heart in his holiness.' In ordinary down-to-earth terms this means that living with oneself, and putting up with one's inadequacies, failures, and miseries, can be a noble work for the glory of God.

170

You have only to move into solitude for a while to realise that living with yourself is harder than you thought. Harder than living with other people. When in isolation, or even when left to yourself with nothing to do, you are very soon brought up face to face with your inherent vanity, your lack of reserves, your tendency to feel sorry for yourself, your shame, your gilt. Indeed unless you have a vocation to solitude, you will find these things growing out of proportion and amounting to a neurosis. Rightly then do St Bernard and the sacred writer of Ecclesiasticus counsel patience with self for the love of God. It is all part of the Canticle's 'ordering of charity within yourself'.

Leaving yourself out of account for the moment, would you not say that something which is made in the image and likeness of God should be reverenced? Would you not say that if it failed as it went along to realize much of this likeness, yet retained the essential resemblance, it should be treated with compassion and given another chance? Would you not say in effect that whatever happened to it, and however much it departed from the looked-for affinity, it should be loved? Now bring yourself back into the argument.

Every human being is worthy of reverence, compassion, and love not because of personal merit but because of the likeness which the soul bears to God: because of what God has put of himself into the soul. The way we sometimes talk, it might be thought that we had made ourselves loveable, that we possessed a certain charm which attracted God's love, even that we owned ourselves and were free to dispose of ourselves at our discretion. *Tuus sum ego* is not a pledge made by a dedicated soul: it states a strictly theological fact. We belong to God more than we belong to ourselves. We are stewards only, and have no proprietary rights; we are not so independent that we may dispose of ourselves as we like. The catechism tells us we are children of God. St Paul goes one better and says we are heirs of God and fellow members of Christ's body. As such we are made worthy of love—even from ourselves.

171

As an echo of the text in Genesis about God making man in his image comes St Paul's statement as to how this is effected: 'We are all transformed into the same image as by the Lord's spirit.' In breathing life into matter God is not merely giving something which will be proper to the individual as a human being—as though God were to say 'I am letting you have a life like other people . . . see that you are worthy of man'—but is giving something of himself as a divine being. He is saying:

'I am letting you have a life like mine . . . see that you are worthy of *me*.' St Paul says further that our transformation by the Lord's spirit is 'from glory to glory'. Such a transition from one glory to another, from natural good to supernatural good, is beyond the power of man to bring about. So it needs the breathing of the Lord's spirit.

This idea of breathing is highly significant in the understanding of our subject. The word 'spirituality' derives from it. God not only breathes his life into us so that we may live to him, but he breathes his prayer into us so that we may pray to him with his prayer. 'Prayer is God's breath in man' says the poet George Herbert, 'returning to its birth.' As we hold our lives in fealty to him, so we pray our prayers in unison with him. 'I live, now not I', because the indwelling of God is my whole life . . . I pray now not I, because the prayer of God is my whole articulation. A key text for the soul of prayer to remember is one from Isaias: 'The word that goes forth from my lips, says the Lord, must not return to me void.'

Our mistake too often is to give our own rendering of the prophet's words, and to say: 'The words that come into my head, says the soul, are mine to multiply.' Whereas in fact I have no words or thoughts or virtues which I can call my own. I have nothing to contribute to the glory of God but what God has lent me for his service. I do not have to invent or create or multiply. My function is much simpler: I have only to co-operate, to let myself be used as a channel for the one-way passage of grace. Love may seem to have two starting points, God's and mine, but when examined is seen to have only one.

172

Looked at historically, the spiritual life would seem to be subject to changes which affect it radically. For example the prayer and penance which were standard among the fathers of the desert bears little relation to present-day practice. Counter-Reformation spirituality is as unlike that of the *aggiornamento* as it is of St Bernard's day and earlier. Are there then fashions in prayer? The answer is that the differences are those of emphasis, and even of semantics, rather than of character. As in the case of dogmatic theology, the swing of reaction can be traced in the tradition of mystical theology. But essential spirituality remains intact, and for two very good reasons: human psychology is recognizably the same over the centuries, and God's grace is a constant.

By way of illustration an axiom which goes back to the earliest period of Christian spirituality and asceticism may be examined in the light of what has been considered in the foregoing pages. *Spernere mundum; spernere sese; spernere nullum.* Despise the world; despise self; despise nothing. ('Spurn' or 'renounce' will do equally well.) On the face of it, and each clause taken separately, you would say that our modern Vatican Council spirituality would want to qualify *spernere mundum*, that Bernardine spirituality would want to qualify *spernere sese*, and that seventeenth century spirituality would be deeply suspicious of *spernere nullum*. Yet the aphorism is as valid to us as it was to the fathers of the desert. And what is more it would have been acceptable, despite accidental modifications, to the spirituality of any period in between.

As a formula for perfection the threefold exhortation is, like St Augustine's 'love and do what you will', open to misinterpretation. Rightly interpreted it covers the whole ground. Certainly the psalmist would have approved. 'All things are vanity: every man living . . . put not your trust in the great of this world': *spernere mundum*. 'I am a worm and no man': *spernere sese*. 'Let all flesh bless his name . . . praise the Lord from the earth . . . pray for the things that are for Jerusalem's peace: abundance for them that love you . . . abundance in your towers': *spernere nullum*.

173

Spernere mundum. To renounce the world in the strict sense, and become a religious, is for the relatively few, but to keep the lure of worldliness at a distance is something to which all are called. 'Love not the world nor the things which are in the world' says St John, 'for if any man loves the world, the charity of the Father is not in him.' And again: 'Whosoever is born of God overcomes the world; and this is the victory which overcomes the world, our faith. Who is he who overcomes the world but he who believes that Jesus is the Son of God?' The world in this sense, as distinct from the world which 'God so loved as to give his onlybegotten Son' to save, must be regarded as the enemy of love, as the idol which the first commandment forbids us to worship. The world at one extreme and charity at the other are leavens: each spreads its influence until the whole is impregnated. If we do not dominate that part of us which is of the world, the world will dominate us.

There is a more subtle kind of world than that which appeals to the senses. Material pleasures can lose their attraction after a time, but the world goes on pulling at us right up to the end. As we get older we find that our vicious inclinations do not need much renouncing: it is rather than they renounce us. On the other hand we never reach the stage when we can congratulate ourselves on being free of what the world stands for. What the world offers to the senses is far from being the whole story.

St Peter was rebuked by our Lord because he 'savoured not the things that are of God but the things that are of men'—the things of the world. Again our Lord at the last supper promised the apostles his peace 'not as the world gives'. It was not because of anything to do with the senses that St Peter was at fault; it was because he was judging Christ's impending passion as a worldly man would judge it—in purely temporal terms. The peace which was Christ's legacy to his friends was not a peace of the senses; it was peace of soul. The world can provide peace of a sort, but because the world does not know God it cannot give true peace. The 'world' in our Lord's mind is something to be renounced by his disciples.

174

The world which has to be renounced by the man of prayer may be a way of acting or speaking or thinking. Of the three the hardest to renounce is the worldly way of thinking. Act and talk can be checked and corrected; thought is more elusive. Without being aware of it a man may come to make his standards those of the world; he may be taking his lead from politics, from the press, from the surrounding culture, from a social pattern, and not from Christ. Christian principle does not exist solely to be called upon in moments of crisis and when the issue is sharply divided between good and evil. Christian principle touches life at every point, just as lack of Christian principle touches life at every point, and in the ordinary run of things it is easy to stumble out of the gospel into the world.

The secularization of endeavour and manners is not a danger which threatens only ecclesiastics; it menaces everyone.

Catholic education is useless unless it trains the mind to resist the argument of the world. People may claim to be uninfluenced by their environment, but everyone is to some extent influenced by his environment, and because man lives in the alien environment conditioned by the fall he has to exercise faith or the atmosphere will choke him. 'This is the victory which overcomes the world, our faith': if we drift we do not overcome.

It must shame us to come across people who possess none of our lofty disdain for the world, who have no thought of God, living far better lives than we. The idea of the 'world' as we think of it does not enter their heads, yet they work and suffer and try to make one another happy, and we have only to look at them to know that they are not as worldly as we. The humbling truth is that there are many men and women in the world who can so give themselves to the lives they lead that God rewards their generosity by removing the ordinary pitfalls. For our part we know the pitfalls, one of which is the world. For as long as we have to live in it, we make it our policy *spernere mundum*. 'Despise' the world? Despise ourselves for being so much of it.

175

Spernere sese. Impossible though it is to disregard self, either in prayer or in anything else that we do, it is perfectly possible to despise self and renounce what we know to be feeding self-love and (that quaint-sounding term) self-esteem. If we know anything at all of ourselves we should have little difficulty in despising what we see. The difficulty lies in distinguishing between the morbid self-hatred which is sterile and the humble self-hatred which is healthy. There are those who feel no self-hatred whatever, and who wonder what all the fuss is about. Let them go on as they are, renouncing themselves where God gives them the light to see what is to be renounced, and above all not trying to work up a sense of guilt about it.

To dangle before oneself the image of a soul worthy to be despised has nothing to do with humility, and may well be a piece of self-dramatization. Since the ideal is to forget oneself —it is better, again to cite St Bernard, to forget oneself than to mortify oneself—it does the soul no good to be reminded of a self which does not exist. All imagined selves are potentially harmful, from the humble to the heroic, because they get in the way of the true and confuse the judgment. Of the two the make-believe heroic soul is less troublesome to the spirit than the make-believe humble soul: he can be more easily exploded.

The despising of self is accordingly an awkward matter to handle. Anything which can become a fetish needs careful treatment, and when the abasement of self is taken up as an experiment in applied mysticism it can lead to much delusion. The maxim *spernere sese* is amply fulfilled where the soul is able to say: 'I am nothing, I can do nothing without God's grace, I know that any ideas of my own are bound to be wrong, I look to God to take my nothingness and make it into something which gives him glory . . . and now the less I think about myself and all this the better.' By all means let me despise myself, but why waste time on this when I can abstract from self and give glory to God? I shall never abstract completely, but then God knows this.

176

Spernere nullum. This third clause may be put into effect only when the other two have been verified. Unless serious effort is made to break down the obstacles of worldliness and selfishness it would be rash to welcome created goods indiscriminately. 'If riches abound' is the psalmist's approach to the question of temporal prosperity, 'set not your heart upon them.' It is not a matter of possession so much as one of desire. That there is nothing wrong with prosperity as such is admitted by the psalmist who promises to the just man and to him who fears the Lord that 'glory and wealth shall be in his house'. The condition is justice and a holy fear of God. Even where there is enjoyment of wealth there has to be a spirit of detachment. If poverty, whether in fact or in spirit, were not important, our Lord would not have made a beatitude of it.

At first it is difficult to square what our Lord said about riches with the above injunction to 'despise nothing'. The camel and the eye of a needle, the rich young man who turned away, the man whose wealth made him insensitive to people like the poor man Lazarus: do not the gospels condemn riches out of hand? Our Lord does not condemn so much as contemn. If material goods are kept in their place they are no obstacle. All created good is God's before it finds its way into man's hands, and in the first book of scripture God has pronounced upon the excellence of his creation. It is what man does with it once he holds it that is the important thing. If he holds it in a loose hand there is no contradiction between *spernere mundum* and *spernere nullum*.

'Every creature of God is good' St Paul reminds Timothy, who seems to have been somewhat strait-laced, 'and nothing is to be rejected that is received with thanksgiving.' Reading this statement without the rest of scripture and the whole of Christian tradition to qualify it, a man might judge that all he has to do is to recite a few words of thanks and that this entitles him to embrace creaturely pleasures without scruple. There can be no free pass to enjoy unlimited pleasure. Thanks or no thanks, the legitimate use of material pleasure is conditioned by the spirit of detachment which preceded, accompanied, and followed its enjoyment.

177

We read with joy how our Lord promised to his disciples a hundredfold of this world's gifts, and in the world to come life everlasting. Here, we think, is complete vindication of *spernere nullum*. When our Lord himself blesses the possession of material things, and lavishly at that, why hesitate? But the question is not altogether closed, because we must note the condition on which the hundredfold is promised: 'Everyone that has left house or brethren or sisters or father or mother or wife or children or lands for my name's sake.' There is an essential relation here between radical renunciation and subsequent possession.

Only when the earthly satisfaction has been surrendered can that state of mind come about which finds in created goods no obstacle to perfection, but if anything a help. When everything is, either tacitly or explicitly, submitted to God for approval, and when the soul is just as ready to do without as to enjoy, there can hardly be much danger. So if St Paul is telling Timothy to take things more easily and to 'drink a little wine for his stomach's sake', it is because he knows his Timothy. He knows that Timothy has renounced himself, and so has satisfied the condition. What happens from now on, whether he takes the wine or not, is immaterial. When everything in the created order is seen to be an object of God's love, and designed for a purpose in his plan, the possible harmfulness is taken out of the surrounding world as a poison is taken out of a snake-bite.

Part of the hundredfold is being able to see all creation—nature and life and suffering and art and happiness and history and people and science—as reflecting God's love, and therefore as worthy of our reverence. Not only as worthy of our reverence but of our engagement. We might find it more satisfactory to unite ourselves with God immediately, and so to serve and enjoy him, but he has arranged that we serve and enjoy him by mediation. The media all about us are invitations to recognize his love. 'If we do not enjoy the things which we see' says Chesterton, 'how shall we enjoy God whom we do not see?'

178

It is more convenient to be told to spurn nothing than to be told to spurn the world and to spurn ourselves. 'The world is full of good things' we can say, 'and I must make the most of them for the glory of God.' If it truly is for the glory of God, then let the statement stand. But often there are 'implications in these ringing sentiments, so that we go on to collect as many of the good things as we can . . . and the glory of God takes second place to the gratification of self. 'St Paul says that whether we eat or drink, we eat or drink to the Lord' is our comforting conclusion, 'therefore the more we eat and drink the better.' There is a fallacy somewhere.

It is no digression to say that the occasions when God grants us a light upon a particular subject are normally followed by a period of interior peace and a sense of simplicity. This is right: grace produces such effects. But experience would seem to show that we can make too much of our interior peace, luxuriating in it, and what is intended to be simplicity can become over-simplification. 'Nothing of value shall ever come forth' wrote Walt Whitman, 'that does not make further struggle necessary.' So it would be a mistake and a waste of God's light if we were to interpret the *spernere nullum* to our own advantage. The advantage to look for in the interpretation of anything, from an invocation to a dogma, is God's.

God derives his own advantage from the light which he sends to the souls of men, but from the point of view of the men there must always, if anything of value is to come forth, be further struggle. Light is not for basking. Nor does the grace of simplicity come to condone the irresponsible. In Proverbs we read how wisdom enriches those who seek after knowledge and love truth. 'I walk in the paths of judgment . . . that I may fill the treasuries of those that know me.' No spurning of good things here. But there are more important things than riches and crowns: 'My fruit is better than gold and precious stones, my flowers than choice silver.' Man has need of this wisdom or he will find that the gold, the precious stones, the choice silver will dazzle him into folly.

179

God in his mercy so often allows us interludes of peace that when the struggle begins again we are tempted to question the wisdom of it. It hardly seems fair, we complain, that we who are trying to serve him in all generosity should be distracted from our main concern, namely prayer, by these recurring and meaningless upsets. But life is meant to be upset, and struggle is far from meaningless. The whole of fallen man's time on earth is a warfare, and it is only because God takes our weakness into account that we are allowed our intervals of peace. We are within our rights to take advantage of a lull, but the normal condition of man is that of battle.

Accordingly we should not be either surprised or dismayed when temptation comes round every corner, when our recollection is shattered, when people misunderstand our motives, when we retreat into loneliness for escape and find only further struggle. Once more it is an occasion for the exercise of faith. The psalmist felt the same weakness and inadequacy but was able to proclaim: 'By you, O God, I shall be delivered from temptation and by your strength I shall scale the wall . . . for God has girt me with his strength . . . my God who teaches my hands to war . . . you have given me the protection of your salvation, your right hand has held me up . . . you have girded me around with strength unto battle.'

We are too close to our own problems and sorrows to be able to see them in perspective. A certain astigmatic tendency has to be allowed for by which crosses become blurred when viewed at close range. As in the case of our prayer, where we are too personally involved to be able to know what is going on, the tactic of this constant warfare eludes us. Just because we are at the centre of it we cannot see the strategy. 'Blessed are they that have not seen but have believed.' The engagement seems to be mounted on such a colossal scale that we feel powerless, dwarfed, defeated. But defeat, like happiness and hope, is an attitude of mind. Defeat is an admission, and until it is given the struggle goes on. For as long as it goes on without the admission, it triumphs.

180

If the struggle were against persecution it would be something straightforward which we would know more or less how to face. We might not feel at all courageous, but at least we would know that it was the will of God, and this in itself would be exhilarating. There is an allure—anyway in the thought of it if not in the concrete—about martyrdom. There is no allure about battling against nerves, depression, tepidity, scruples. Though the sense of challenge is completely absent here, the need to resist is just as great as in the case of suffering persecution. Heroism is a dream; insufficiency is an actuality. Heroism has its moments; insufficiency has its years.

These inner conflicts, in which temptation and melancholy replace the sword and dungeon, can drive us, unless we are careful, in upon ourselves. They are meant to draw us out towards God in trust, but they can easily, particularly in an age which probes into the secrets of the mind, make introverts of us and so may restrict the operation of grace. Though science comes forward with its psychotherapy to help us in getting hold of ourselves—psychotherapy being the Greek for cure of the soul—what we really need is more faith. We need to know that God is vitally interested in us as individuals, that he knows all about our condition which he has himself allowed, that his grace is enabling us to bear the trial even if it is not his will to end it immediately.

The nightmare of guilt, the dread of the next thing to happen, the fear that the judgment will unearth infidelities about which we are powerless to do anything, the conviction that whatever we are doing now, whether or not it has to do with the service of God, is sinful: these are compulsion-neuroses. It may not help to know what they are, but it should help to know that *God* knows what they are and that his mercy and love are unaffected by them. We are always told that there is only one cure for scruples: the combination of absolute obedience and blind trust. This is true, but it so happens that when the trial of scruples is at its worst the act of surrender is the most difficult of all to make. Difficult but not impossible. Therein lies the value of the trial.

181

Scruples are evidence of pride, not of humility. The scrupulous man may be meticulous, but he is also obstinate. He has an opinion of his own; he decides that everyone is wrong but himself. It is not that he cannot obey—it is his obedience to some things that makes him meticulous—but that he will not humble himself and trust to the judgment of another. He claims to be obeying the voice of his conscience, but in fact he is obeying the voice of self. Even when he admits that his conscience may be misguided, and that the conscience of authority may be guide enough for other people, he prefers to act on his own conscience, right or wrong, because he knows it and does not dare go back on it. Pride first, fear second. Against this combination only complete surrender in faith can win.

What God wants of the soul is not this or that outward observance, but surrender. Once the soul has surrendered, once the root obstinacy has been replaced by an admission that self cannot be trusted and that God can, then grace can take over and be the undisputed guide of conscience. So long as scruples are indulged as a sign of piety, and not resisted as a sign of selfishness, grace has no room to work. Scruples are not an adjunct to devotion and zeal: they are a temptation, and unless they are recognised as such they will spread and cramp the spirit.

That scruples are the lot of the devout and not of the godless is no argument for their respectability. It is simply that in the nature of the case the devout are surrounded by ready-made occasions of scrupulosity whereas the godless are not. The godless have put themselves outside the range of conscience, wrong or right. While it may seem more reprehensible to give in to the grosser temptations than to indulge in a niggling little thing like scruples, the point is that any clinging to one's own will when authority shows God's will to be otherwise is not a niggling little thing. The grosser temptations are at least frank about themselves: they do not pretend to be niggling little things. Self-confessed sinners call a sin a sin. It is the devout who mistake sin for scruple and scruple for sin. As always it is a question of searching in faith for truth. The soul that truly seeks God will not stay confused for long.

182

Scruples are different from many other interior temptations and trials in that the occasions of giving in to them cannot be altogether avoided. Occasions are everywhere and threaten every virtue. When suffering from the affliction a soul cannot do anything properly, because every act is distracted by the fear of having sinned over the act performed immediately before. The result is an almost unbroken self-questioning which in turn leads to nervous strain and an inability to look forward to anything or to see an end of the difficulty. The soul must resolutely not look back, and in regard to the future must practise the most determined hope. Obedience and grace will do the rest.

But what about those other interior trials: melancholy, listlessness, restlessness, loneliness, and the sense of grievance? The first thing is, as in the case of scruples, to recognise them as temptations as well as trials. Where occasions for scruple are so manifold as to reduce the possibility of direct attack, the occasions which induce melancholy and the rest can be squarely faced and side-stepped. Admittedly there will always be circumstances in a person's life over which he has no control, and which will cause sadness. Whatever he does to prepare for it and fight against it, there must be times when a loss or a parting or a disappointment is bound to make a man miserable. These occasions are allowed for and have to be met head-on. We cannot insure ourselves, and are not meant to, against the hazards of life with their necessary suffering.

There is all the difference between necessary suffering sent by God and unnecessary suffering wallowed in by us. It is the mood of melancholy, not prompted by anything in particular, which must be looked upon as an occasion of sin and broken up. Why are we depressed, sorry for ourselves, longing for change (any sort of change), unwilling to give ourselves to our work and to other people? If there is a specific cause, it must be looked at and dealt with rationally. If there is no specific cause, the mood may well be a trial allowed by God, but it is also a source of temptation. In the ordinary way God does not will us to be sad, and if we are sad through our own fault it is an imperfection.

183

Allowing that most of us are egocentric, we can nevertheless prevent ourselves from being haunted by our egos. The ego distorts the vision of those who might otherwise see straight. Though we cannot help seeing ourselves in whatever we do, we should be able to see through ourselves. Seeing straight means looking towards God and seeing what lies between in relation to him. If our focus is on God, we shall see melancholy, listlessness, restlessness and so on for what they are, and not be deceived by them. It will then be a matter of common prudence: we shall resist whatever incites us to their indulgence.

Where more outward failings are at stake we appreciate the necessity of erecting barriers and establishing safeguards. Take the case of a man who drinks too much and too often. Though we need not consider here the man who is technically an alcoholic, the one whose condition amounts to a disease, we can include the potential alcoholic. During the time before he became a subject for the doctor—and in the life of even the most authenticated alcoholic there must have been such a time —had he the power to resist the tendency, and if so how did he use it? *Mutatis mutandis,* melancholy and kindred evils are in the same situation. Depression may be a disease, but there must have been a time when it was not. Did the potential depressive avoid the occasions of gloom, take steps to shake off his mood, try to live more positively and altruistically? Or did he say (with quite a number of alcoholics): 'This is a disease, and there is nothing I can do about it',

Granted that diseases may be latent, it is surely still true that if they never declare themselves *at all* they are not really (anyway to the lay mind) diseases. We may be prone to sadness, we may be more sensitive and vulnerable than others, we may be short on vitality, but if we counter these weaknesses as we would counter the tendency to alcoholic excess we do not end up as their victims. In his degree *everyone* is an embryonic depressive, *everyone* likes change, *everyone* has congenital

leanings towards the line of least resistance. But these things
are not just left to take their course.

184

A factor frequently overlooked by those who hanker after
a particular kind of happiness which is not theirs, after a security, a work, a social circle or a place, is that they may not be
in the mood for it when they get it. They may be out of tune.
They think that they will be at home at last, and then the
home turns out to be a lonely wilderness, a desert. The truth is
that man has only a limited knowledge of his psychological and
emotional reactions to given stimuli, so that when he projects
himself in imagination into an external environment which
attracts him, he is dealing with the unpredictable. He is seeing
only what he wants to see, and what his senses tell him is desireable. He is seeing, as though looking at it in a mail-order
catalogue, an agreeable setting for specified goods. He is for-
getting the all-important factor, namely his own individual
psyche.

It is one of our human flaws that we too closely relate the
external to the internal, and conclude from this false identifi-
cation that if we can secure the external and wrap it round
ourselves we have thereby secured the internal. 'Give me certain conditions' we say, 'and I shall be nice and snug for the
rest of my days.' We are forever reaching out for the ideal, and
it is right that we should, but it is a mistake to think that by
making a few adjustments of a practical kind we shall find the
ideal dropping into our lap. In an effort to fuse the ideal with
the physically attainable we sometimes break out of the frame
in which God has set us and put ourselves in another.

Spiritual and psychological problems are rarely settled by
physical, and still less by geographical, solutions. When we try
to satisfy our ever-questing spirit by making a substantial
change in the setting of our lives, we find more often than not
that we have miscalculated and that there is a substantial discrepancy. The psyche does not match the setting. The mood,
unaccountably, is wrong. The ideal life was not what we
thought it was after all . . . so where do we go now? To recover
from a significant blunder calls for humility. We have to tell
God, and ourselves, that he was right and that we were not.

185

At the root of most of our mistakes in the ordering of our lives lies a mistaken notion of cause and effect. For example we think that money makes for security, that health makes for happiness, that education makes for self-confidence, that position and success make for self-fulfilment. We probably do not question these assumptions unless something drastic happens to us which forces us to revise our values. We read books and see plays which challenge these propositions, but in our hearts we remain unaffected. We are not going to think again unless experience forces us to, and we hope that experience will leave us alone on these issues. To think in this way would seem to be a rational, and even prudent, way of thinking. The trouble is that it is too rational, too tidy, too simple. Gullibly, we have reached conclusions prompted by the wisdom of the world— and a not very penetrating wisdom at that.

What this does is to leave out the supremely important element of human existence, namely the providence of God. Life refuses to be cut up and sold in packages. Anyone can see how foolish it would be to say: 'I have got what I want, so now I can be happy.' Yet it is not considered foolish to go on trying to get what one wants so as to be happy. Or at all events to salvage whatever happiness is going. On the occasions when one has fought one's way to a certain goal and finally possessed it, what is the result? Satisfaction for a time perhaps, but not for long. Other goals have to be proposed, and other fights embarked upon. As a rule it is the struggle to get there that is more satisfying than what one has wanted to enjoy on arrival.

In this life nothing is stable except the will of God. 'In my abundance I said: I shall never be moved' confesses the psalmist, and then what happens? 'You turned away your face from me, Lord, and I became troubled.' The swing is from one extreme to another, and not necessarily because of outward circumstances but more because of something which takes place within. 'In the evening shall be tears, and in the morning gladness.' Or it may be the other way round. We cannot tell which it will be, because we vary from day to day.

186

Our Lord says clearly enough where unstable man can expect to find stability. In him, and by faith. He says that instead of building upon sand we can build upon a rock. He says that if our first objective in life is the kingdom of God we do not have to worry about other things, which are variables, because we shall possess the only thing which is constant. In the midst of contingencies, and things which depend upon contingencies, we are given the chance of resting upon a foundation which is permanent. The sole condition is faith. And even this is provided for us by God.

The kingdom of God is not subject to change, and this kingdom we can possess within us. This kingdom is eternal, and already in this life we are introduced to its eternity. 'This is eternal life' said our Lord in his prayer to the Father, 'that they may know you, the only true God, and Jesus Christ whom you have sent.' In granting us knowledge of himself, Father and Son, he has granted us something which no outward force can take from us, and which even our own unreliable emotions cannot alter so long as in the will we remain faithful. Left to ourselves we are at the mercy of our emotions, but we are not left to ourselves. 'I in them and you in me' our Lord goes on to pray, 'that the love wherewith you have loved me may be in them, and I in them.'

Our Lord makes it clear, moreover, that his prayer was not for the apostles alone. 'Not for them only do I pray' he says, 'but for them also who through their word shall believe in me.' The word has been preached, the grace of faith has been granted, God has established his presence in our souls. Our Lord tells us how we may maintain ourselves in this grace: 'Abide in me, and I in you . . . abide in my love.' Because it seems so simple we feel that the summons must entail more, and we wonder if we have missed some key clause. But if our Lord's words mean anything at all, life in him *is* simple. Often he tells his disciples not to be anxious, not to be solicitous, not to be fearful. It is fear that makes complications of what is meant to be simple. The doctrine is simple enough; it is the response that too often is not.

187

Taken in its most necessary sense, as obliging all Christians, the words 'abide in me and I in you' mean remaining in a state of grace. The life in Christ which begins at baptism is meant to be an abiding reality to the soul. For too many it is merely a doctrine and not an actuality which deepens with day to day experience. Life in Christ is love, and love is meaningless unless it is experienced. A man does not love merely by signing a testimonial which makes love a necessary requisite. Love which is not experienced is like beauty which is not seen, like truth which is not known, like goodness which is not practised. So the words 'abide in me and I in you' are a summons to work upon the state of grace, and not merely to exist in it. While to preserve the state of grace satisfies the obligation, who would say that we are called to do only what is obligatory?

Though love has to be experienced to be worthy of the name, it does not have to be experienced all the time. A grace strictly extraordinary would be needed if the soul were to enjoy the *affectus* of love habitually. St Bernard describes how the soul, until perfect love is possessed which is 'wholly divine', no sooner has a taste of the real thing than 'the needs of the flesh solicit it, the weakness of corruption cannot sustain it, and above all fraternal love recalls it'. These cares which pull at the soul's ascent are what the saint calls a *proprium* which is only to be expected in the prayer of one who is not yet wholly purified of sensible things.

Since charity is essentially spiritual in character, it cannot be accurately measured by the works which it inspires. This poses a problem, because if it is spiritual it can arrive at union only in the spirit. What then of outward action? The answer must be that for as long as man lives his life on earth, he develops the interior actuation of love by means of exterior works. He is not yet spiritualized, so the essential union to which his charity tends has to be delayed until he is. In the meantime he can arrive at a real, though necessarily incomplete, union with our Lord and with the members of his mystical body.

188

'True love' says St Bernard, cannot be fruitless.' So if we

love in Christ we are making a substantial contribution to the welfare of the mystical body, helping it to grow till it reaches full stature in Christ. What makes this fruition of our love possible is the fact that Christ is loving in us and with us. The Father's kingdom on earth is extended by the joint action of his Son and of those who are living in his Son. By performing charitable acts we can help a little, but by being one with charity itself we can do far more.

This interior union with charity is not a piece of spiritual dexterity. 'Now watch carefully . . . I am going to unite myself with charity and you will see what happens.' Sleight of hand may be an advantage in the outer fringe of religion, and we need to be pretty nimble to gain all the indulgences that are going, but to be admitted to the heart of charity itself is not like being admitted in audience to a high ecclesiastic. In the first place the initiative is taken by God and not by us, and in the second place it is an exchange which keeps its fruitfulness secret. If the initiative were left to us, it would mean that God would have to wait upon our decision; and if the fruitfulness were visible it would mean that we would tend to appropriate to ourselves the credit for the work.

In his wisdom God does not allow us to see much of what goes on in the soul under the action of grace. This is not only to prevent us from feeling we were doing all the work but also to keep us from interfering. If we could follow what was being done we would think of a better way of doing it, and get in the way. Grace must have a free hand, and the only means of securing this is to have us bound, gagged, and blindfold from the start. In the most significant activity of life, namely love, our natural reactions are at fault: instinctively we judge it by its emotional content. If it does not register emotionally we are doubtful about the quality of our love. The same in the case of prayer: it is feelings which we think must count. So because we are apt to cling to our illusions about love and prayer, even after we have been told and when we ought to know better, God takes us out of harm's way and lets us see nothing.

189

'He who loves God is present to God to the degree in which he loves.' This statement of St Bernard's should convince us, if nothing else does, of the futility of trying to find out how far we have got in the spiritual life. Only God knows the quality of our love, and he is not going to tell us what it is. Only God knows how present we are to him, and again he is not going to say. There are times when we *feel* very close to him indeed, and when we *feel* that our love must be mounting, but what do these feelings tell us except that we are in a good mood and that if we are wise we must not bank on having them tomorrow?

So once again it has to be a matter of faith. Faith knows the difference between the experience of love and the feeling of it, between the reality of prayer and the warmth of it. St Paul prays for the Ephesians that they be strengthened by God's spirit with might unto the inward man, and 'that Christ may dwell by faith in your hearts'. It would be no good his dwelling there by feeling, because by tomorrow the feeling might be gone and he would have no place to dwell in. Nor may he dwell by imagination, because the picture we form would not only depend upon our skill but would in any case be inaccurate. Not by memory, because neither have we seen him nor could we remember all that we have read and heard about him. Not by intellectual ability, because again the opportunity of housing Christ within ourselves would not be open to all. So if Christ is to dwell at all in our hearts, it must be by faith. Only then are we sure of being 'strengthened with might unto the inward man' by God's spirit.

With what result? The text goes on to tell us: 'That being rooted and founded in charity, you may be able to comprehend, with all the saints, what is the breadth and length and height and depth.' The indwelling of Christ by faith *means* being rooted and founded in charity. Charity and faith go together, and it is God's spirit which plants them in the inward man. Nor is this all. 'To know also the charity of Christ which surpasses all knowledge, that you may be filled unto all the fulness of God.' The charity of Christ surpasses not only knowledge but everything else: it is the 'fulness of God.'

190

If the experience of love is not the feeling of love, what is it? Certainly the distinction is not immediately obvious. Nor would it be quite fair to explain it by saying that if a man can be stupid without feeling stupid, can be diseased without feeling ill, can be old without feeling old, then there is nothing to prevent a man loving and not feeling that he loves. The point here, in the experience of love as distinct from the emotional glow of love, is that the soul chooses the love of God and neighbour regardless of what, having chosen, it is going to feel like. Being stupid, being diseased, being old are not states which are chosen. By deliberately setting himself to love, a man loves. If feelings accompany the act, so much the nicer for him. But feelings are not the condition on which the choice is made, nor the infallible sign that the authentic activity is going on.

It is significant in this connection that we are *commanded* by God to love. 'Thou shalt love the Lord thy God . . . thou shalt love they neighbour as thyself . . . this is my commandment, that you love one another.' God does not command us to feel love, because he knows that we might not be able to obey. He does not even command us to try our best to feel love, because a forced emotion is little better than a pretended emotion, and in any case could not be kept up. So he orders us simply to love, because the act of the will which agrees to obey love's summons is something which can be kept up continuously, and which does not cease unless repudiated deliberately by a contrary act—an act of serious sin.

This is borne out by our Lord's words which immediately follow the commandment that we love one another as he has loved us. 'Greater love than this no man has, that he lay down his life for his friends.' The laying down of life represents a cool, deliberate, heroic, but matter of fact, choice. If our Lord had said that love's greatest act was ecstatic prayer or overwhelming human affection for another, we might believe him but we would know at once that such burning loves were out of reach for us. But he did not say this. He said something significantly different. He was talking about the will. In describing the highest act of love he instanced willingness to sacrafice self.

191

In fairness, we must present the other side, and try to account for it. In *Parochial and Plain Sermons* Cardinal Newman wrote: 'Let us pray God to give us *all* graces . . . the *beauty* of holiness, which consists in tender and eager affection towards our Lord and Saviour; which is, in the case of the Christian, what beauty of person is to the outward man, so that through God's mercy our souls may have, not strength and health only, but a sort of bloom and comeliness; and that as we grow older in body, we may, year by year, grow more youthful in spirit.' Clearly the tenor of this paragraph is the recommendation of religious emotion. But before we conclude that for Newman true devotion consisted in pious sentiment, we should note that demonstrative affection towards the person of Christ is something, as is shown in the first line of the quotation, which he prays for as a grace. Quite justifiably he is asking God for something extra; he is not pronouncing upon the bedrock essence of love.

Also it should be borne in mind that spirituality in Newman's time tended to be more flowery—anyway in its expression —and that men like Newman and Father Faber worked, and presumably prayed, along somewhat different lines than would be normal today. The spiritual doctrine which has been preached in England by Father Stuart, Father Considine, Abbot Chapman, Father Gerald Vann, and in America by Father Merton, is less concerned with the heart than with the intellect and will. This is not to belittle the nineteenth century spiritual writers; it is merely to point out the shift of emphasis, and to allow also for what may have been differences of temperament.

It is worth observing here that our Lord, when he lays down a doctrine, makes no demand for feelings but only for acceptance and obedience. 'Take ye and eat. This is my body . . . do this for a commemoration of me . . . not everyone that says to me, Lord, Lord, shall enter into the kingdom of heaven, but he that does the will of my Father . . . my flesh is meat indeed, my blood is drink . . . whose sins you shall forgive, they are forgiven.' Nothing about requiring an emotional response in all this. What he wants is consent, borne out in action.

192

Many of our Lord's statements possess a directness about them, a take-it-or-leave-it quality, which is particularly refreshing to us who are accustomed to the more cautious pronouncements of preachers and spiritual writers. Our Lord does not qualify with terms such as 'figuratively speaking' and 'it might be true to say' and 'almost as if'. He says the thing straight out, and his hearers either believe him or move on. This is especially the case when he gives information which it would be possible for him to know only if he were God. 'Go, your sins are forgiven', 'your faith has made you whole', 'I know the Father because I am from him and he has sent me', 'before Abraham was, I am', 'he that sees me sees the Father also'. Texts could be multiplied, each one a clear positive announcement calculated to shock people into thinking.

One such statement can be taken here as standing for the rest. 'Where two or three are gathered together in my name, there am I in the midst of them.' In the first place we note what he did not say, but which, had he been man only and not God, would have been a more credible thing to say. Thus he did not say that when his friends were assembled in his memory, it would be just as though he were present among them. 'You must imagine me kneeling there with you . . . you must think of me in heaven praying for you . . . you will feel the influence of my love and will be comforted . . . if you try hard enough you will meet me at this mystical level . . . I shall be with you in spirit.'

What in fact he did say was that he would be among them. It was a promise and not a vague hope. It was not conditioned by either the sentiments of devotion on the part of those assembled in his name or on the Father's willingness to put the suggestion into effect. Since he was God he could make what guarantees he wished, and on whatever terms he wished. The terms were simply that his disciples come before him together and in faith: he would be there. He did not even demand special prayers. That they should arrange to gather in his name would be enough. His grace would prompt them as to what to do and say when the time came.

193

Having considered some of the implications arising from our Lord's words 'Where two or three are gathered together in my name, there am I in the midst of them', we can briefly review the text in relation to the theology of grace. This should come as a help in the work of prayer, so is not theological speculation for itself's sake. The point to be appreciated is that Christ's presence does not depend upon people assembling together in one place, but rather the other way about: they assemble because the grace of his presence has drawn them together in his name. If this were not so it makes God wait upon the will or whim of man. To think of Christ's presence being summoned to a particular spot, hitherto unoccupied by his presence, on account of two or three people who have either planned to meet or who happen to meet is to suggest something magical.

There is nothing magical about the doctrine of God's presence in his creatures, either collectively or individually. He is present in inanimate matter because it derives its being from him; he is more present in the souls of those who are in the state of grace because his spirit *is* grace; he is present still more when such souls address him in prayer. Applied to our text we see how the divine presence must be among souls who are in charity with one another and who come together in the name of Christ. Love insures God's presence because it *is* God's presence. Souls who are out of charity, who have cut themselves off from grace by mortal sin, may assemble together as much as they like but they are not assembling in his name.

It is because of St John's cardinal text—'God is love, and he who lives in charity lives in God, and God in him'—that the life of grace becomes intelligible to us. It becomes clear to us now that whenever we are moved to do a good act, we are in fact, whether we know it or not, moved by love. Not by *our* love, as though it were something of our own, but by his. So of course when two or three of us are together, sharing the same purpose and in charity with one another, Christ who is already in us—and who as God is in all creation—is very particularly and really in our midst.

194

Writing to the Thessalonians, St Paul asks that 'the Lord direct your hearts in the charity of God and the patience of Christ'. This is no mere formal salutation, a farewell message. St Paul is thinking of supernatural qualities which exist in the soul by the grace of the Holy Spirit, and praying that the Thessalonians may allow them to develop. That the Lord will direct the hearts of his faithful in his own virtues if the faithful lay themselves open to his action is certain. The Holy Spirit is the sanctifier, and the way in which the sanctifier operates in souls is by eliciting human reflections of divine attributes.

About charity the situation is clear. If God dwells in the

baptised soul by the power of his grace, then charity, since God is charity, must be present. So far as charity is concerned, it is now a question, as St Paul tells the Thessalonians, of letting the Lord direct the heart. When it comes to the virtue of patience the situation is somewhat different. Scripture says that God is charity, but it does not say that he is patience. St Paul makes a distinction between the charity of the Father and the patience of the Son.

We think of patience as such a human virtue that it goes better with our concept of Christ than with our concept of God the Father. The Father is patient in the sense that he puts up with man's infidelity and awaits his repentance, but we do not think of him practising patience any more than we think of him practising humility. But we do think of Christ practising patience. The gospels supply abundant evidence of Christ's patience, and, reading between the lines, we can judge how patient he must have been with his disciples, let alone with his persecutors. St Paul asks that our hearts may be directed in Christ's kind of patience. If we think of patience only as not getting annoyed, we think of it inadequately. Endurance? Certainly patience means endurance. But looked at from God's point of view, patience is a facet of charity. The truly patient man so loves as not to get annoyed, so loves as to endure.

195

Our Lord said that we were to learn of him because he was 'meek and humble of heart'. Again qualities which we do not apply to the Father but which are imitable as possessed by the Son. What, first of all, is this meekness which we are told to reproduce? It is evidently an important virtue not only because Christ himself was meek but also because he made it one of the beatitudes. Clearly it has nothing to do with the obsequious shrinking which the word has come to mean. If meekness meant not taking a firm line it would be the last trait to characterise our Lord. In associating it with servility of manner we miss its true nature, which is best understood as the antithesis of arrogance, boastfulness, ostentation. Meekness does not thrust itself forward, does not seek applause, but at the same time does not evade the responsibility of taking a lead when a principle is at stake.

The meekness which did not prevent our Lord from disputing as a child with the theologians in the temple, and as man from publicly exposing the faults of various respected classes in Jerusalem, was proof against personal glorification. He resisted the attempts of his followers to make him king, and only so as to remind the Jews of prophecy and of his messianic mission did he allow the demonstration with palms and singing on the occasion of his entry into the city at the beginning of Holy Week. Indeed since he knew what was to follow, and how his disciples were to scatter, this triumphal procession bore witness to his meekness rather than to anything else.

It should not be difficult to estimate how far we follow our Lord's example in meekness. Does lack of recognition and gratitude bother me, or am I content to escape notice? Am I bewitched by rank, titles, the society of the great, or am I just as much at home among the humble? Do I steer the conversation into channels which will allow me to show my knowledge, by gifts as a talker, my rare virtues, or am I ready to listen? Do I evade tiresome and somewhat menial duties on grounds of health, position, age, having more important work to do . . . when it would be more honest to say that I am lazy and that I feel myself to be superior? Meekness becomes harder and more subtle as one grows older.

196

The problem presents itself as to how Christ, knowing he was divine as well as human, could in any real sense be 'humble of heart'. The answer is twofold: in the first place humility is truth, and in the second it is a necessary accompaniment of charity as possessed in this life. Christ's humility could suffer no loss by his claim to be the Son of God, because he *was* the Son of God. It would have been untrue and a piece of affectation had he denied it. Until he was born, the humblest person who had ever lived was his mother, and she proclaimed, without a shadow falling across her humility, that from henceforth all generations would call her blessed.

In his human nature Christ experienced, only without imperfection, the emotions and temptations which are the lot of the rest of us. His virtues too, only possessed perfectly, were those common to man. Himself perfect charity, he enjoyed the perfect humility which went with it. Had he not been perfectly humble he would have been vulnerable to the vice directly opposed to humility. Pride however—though the temptation to this the most serious of all sins was evident in three of its aspects when he had fasted for forty days on the mountain—found no place in him. Nor could it do, if by his obedience and humility he was to counterbalance and atone for the disobedience and pride of Adam.

To the Philippians St Paul writes of the nature of Christ's humility, 'who being in the form of God, thought it not robbery to be equal with God, but emptied himself [*The New English Bible* has 'made himself nothing'], taking the form of a servant, being made in the likeness of men and in habit found as a man. He humbled himself, becoming obedient unto death, even to the death of the cross.' How closely the two virtues, humility and charity, are linked can be seen by the way in which St Paul gives this exposition of our Lord's humility immediately after saying 'each one not considering the things that are his own but those that are other men's', and urging that 'this mind be in you which was also in Christ Jesus'. And from the Old Testament: 'Love mercy and walk humbly' wrote Micheas, 'with your God.'

197

God made man for his own sake, but he became man for ours. The Word became flesh not only to redeem the human race from sin, not only to establish a Church which was to take his place and continue his work after his death, not only to fulfil prophecy and perfect the Old Law, but also to be a practical pattern for us individually in our everyday lives. In New Testament terms to 'love mercy and walk humbly with God' is, in the words of St Paul, to 'walk in Christ'. 'Put you on' he says again, 'the Lord Jesus Christ.' To what extent do we obey St Paul's injunction, and make Christ our living and imitable model?

From the four gospels and twenty-one epistles we are meant to conclude that religion for us is trying to make Christ's life and our own coincide. It is letting one life emerge instead of two. If this sounds utterly unreal and fanciful—a devout whimsical concept suitable for edification but not for action—it means that we have confined our attention to the historical figure. The facts of Christ's life are given not for antiquarian study or theological speculation but for the union of *my* life with *his*. Christ's life has somehow, with the help of the sacraments and sanctifying grace *and* the scriptures, to find itself reproduced in the context of my own life. His life must become my centre of gravity.

The objection that our contemporary setting, with its values vastly different from those of Palestine in our Lord's time, makes of such a transposition nothing but a fiction is simply not valid. Differences of time and place and culture do not come into it, and to believe that they do is to be deceived by the localization fallacy. It is, again in the words of St Paul, 'Jesus Christ yesterday, today, and the same for ever'. St Paul was not pointing out that the Second Person of the Blessed Trinity was eternal, a fact which his readers knew already, but that since he stood outside time Christ could re-live his life in every generation and within the circumstances of every Christian life. For what other purpose do the sacraments exist? What other meaning can terms like 'reflecting the Passion' and being 'risen with Christ' possibly have? 'Dwelling in Christ', and he in us, must be possible of realization or the doctrine is meaningless.

198

Either we serve the dead Christ or we serve the living Christ. We cannot serve two Masters. Though we may love and reverence the dead Christ, unless we go on to love and reverence the living Christ we are serving a memory and not an actuality. It is the difference between hero-worship and an existing relationship. Here and now we are related, personally and vitally, so the opportunity is ours to make this relationship the most important thing in life. Given the freedom of our thinking, judging, deciding, this relationship can so develop as to change our whole horizon. The insignificant becomes significant, the haphazard receives direction, the casual contact is a summons of charity. This is only to be expected if we accept the words 'Behold, I make all things new'.

Faith needs to be on the alert if it is not to miss the indications of God's personal involvement with us at every moment. All that happens to us, every detail that we notice in our own small world, represents a providential movement in the much wider movement of God's providence. The course of history is not plotted by chance, nor is the course of our own time on earth. This should not make us fatalistic, as though everything were determined beforehand and nothing we did could alter it, but, allowing for the mystery of God's will, it should make us increasingly sensitive to the implications of commonplace circumstance.

By God's activity the world not only came into being but now exists, grows older, draws nearer to the divinely appointed time of its dissolution. Theologians tell us that even inanimate matter, since Christ is at the heart of God's creation and nodal to it, in some way reflects the mystery of the Incarnation. Everything consequently, and not only sufferings and joys and the things of religion, should speak to us of Christ. At times they may speak to us more of his absence than of his presence, but even here our faith will hold us to the search. The sad part of it is we can go for so long missing his presence—like tires spinning aimlessly without an axle along a road. Christ is our centre, and the whole of life must turn on him.

199

In the end we are down to belief in the fundamental claim: 'I am the way, the truth, and the life, and no man comes to the Father but by me.' Christ's life and Christ's truth are not separate entities: he is the living truth. It is because we cannot come to the Father but by him that Christ and the way are one: he is the true living way. This is not a juggling with words; it is a simple statement of fact. If we understand what is meant by the divine and human nature of Christ, we should be able to see how Christ does embody in himself the only way, the whole truth, the fulness of life. If we were to find ourselves among savages who had never heard of Christianity, we would do well to put to them this doctrine before all else.

What then? Then that God is charity, and that those who live in charity live in God and God in them. Souls that have accepted this much must see how Christ, being God, is love personified. It follows that love must be the way for man to go, the truth for man to seek, the life for man to live. God has chosen love to be the way because his Son is love. He has chosen to reveal his truth in Christ because the mind of man must grope its way towards truth, and in finding Christ it finds truth. He has chosen to give Christ's life to man because without it man would still be under the curse of original sin.

Life is worth living only in so far as it is the life which God means us to live, and this for us Christians is life in Christ. Life lived apart from Christ is an anomaly, a travesty. It is no life at all, and for this reason the soul that is in a state of mortal sin is accounted dead. Life assumes value only in that it reflects the life of Christ. Which, again, is the life of love. If being in a state of grace means no more to us than not being in a state of mortal sin, we are missing the implications of living in Christ, and so of living in love. Who has not experienced the sudden shock of seeing what life is all about, what love is for, what now is expected of one? The vision fades but Christ remains, who is the way, the truth, and the life.

200

For most of us it is only an occasional glimpse of truth that we are allowed, but it is enough to draw into unity as by a single thread the scattered elements of religion. Barren beliefs are barren no longer; speculations are seen to have direction; trials and doubts are understood to have purpose; hopes are not forlorn after all, and longings will find eventually their appropriate satisfaction. Charity is the thread which links everything together. St Paul uses a stronger metaphor and calls it the bond of perfection. Love is the impulse and end at the same time, the *alpha* and *omega,* the first and the last. If for the saint it is the whole of life, worked out in practice from day to day and from hour to hour, for us it should at least be the whole of our intention. It should be that to which we bring our hesitations when looking for a standard to go by, it should be that against which we measure our infidelities, it should be that which provides our incentive in our dealings with others.

From infancy we have been taught the importance of the ten commandments. The decalogue is at once our mandate from God, the ground of our service, the definition of our perfection. It is the frame within which God's will and ours must coincide. If we refuse to bow our will to God's will as revealed in the ten commandments we are outcasts. The decalogue is as fundamental as that. Yet when our Lord is asked about which commandment ranks highest, he says that the whole law is comprised in the twofold precept of love: love of God with the whole heart, soul, mind, and strength, and the love of neighbour as oneself

Only when the reality of love is brought home to us do we see the emptiness of un-love. We may talk about this or that being 'the saddest thing in the world', but strictly the saddest thing is the cutting off of love. Fortunately love dies hard, but such is the power of man's freewill that it can be killed. People are evil only when in one way or another they are denying love. All sin is a negation of love. Death is a potential enemy only in that it can come upon one who has rejected finally his right to love. To those that love, death comes as an ally. 'Come, Lord Jesus.'